Housing PhilanthroInvesting:

Invest with a Purpose

Grow your capital
while helping families own their home

Ivan Anz

Praise for PhilanthroInvesting

Kevin Harrington, As Seen on TV Founder; Original Shark on Shark Tank

"I have personally met Ivan and listened to Ivan's presentation, one on one. His passion for what he does in helping recover the American Dream with his investment system is outstanding. This PhilanthroInvesting system is a "must learn" for any person wanting to grow their capital while helping others."

Darren Jacklin, Board of Directors eXp Realty

"As a High Net Worth Individual (HNWI), I get approached frequently about all different types of investment opportunities. I say NO to most of them as they do not pass my thorough due diligence process.

"What caught my attention with PhilanthroInvesting is that I am able to protect my downside and mitigate exposure to potential risks and liabilities. It holds my investments legally structured while growing my capital and helping others. What more can one ask for?

"As a High Net Worth Investor, I am always qualifying my time, in regard to who I spend time with and what information I take in. Equity & Help, Inc. is fully transparent, and anyone should seriously consider diversifying their portfolio of investments using this Housing Business model. It is a win for the families, a win for the investor and a win for Equity & Help, Inc.

"I am very impressed with their monthly detailed reporting. I have consistently been earning double-digit returns, hassle-free without the need of investing a lot of time and effort. My intention is to become the first City Hero with Equity & Help, Inc. and to become the Canadian Founder of Equity & Help, Inc. in Canada.

"As a successful real estate investor, this creative and ingenious business model is a must-read for beginners who want to learn about the housing business without the headaches of a landlord, or even if you are a seasoned veteran. I guarantee that you will not find another model as unique and as exceptional as this one."

Mike Calhoun, BOARD OF ADVISORS; Founder & CEO "World's Greatest Mastermind"

"Fortunately, I have personally had the opportunity to work with Ivan on various levels; he is a true leader, gentleman, and compassionate business developer. His implementation of systems and professionalism is profound, while keeping equally focused on the benefits to his PhilanthroInvestors and most importantly new homeowners."

Tatiana Mersiadis, CEO, LY2NK Foundation

"In just a few short years Equity & Help, Inc. has already created an impressive track record in helping hundreds of families across the U.S.

"What drew me in is Ivan Anz's character. He has dedicated his life to a cause greater than himself. His life demonstrates results, as well as being heart-centered and he lives his life in integrity. That is the type of person I want to do business with and a cause I believe in.

"We have gone through a thorough due diligence process and have determined that Equity & Help's track record, accountability and reporting is of the highest caliber. We now are acquiring a portfolio of Housing with freedom and ease, stabilizing families while multiplying wealth and leaving behind the headaches of a landlord!

"Our private group of companies is committed to helping over 1,000 families in order to help achieve Equity & Help's goal of helping 10,000 Families by 2025.

"Giving people a second chance and making a difference in raising the conscious level of help in the investment world is a responsibility we all need to take on. Equity & Help helps me fulfill these values."

Linda V. Ferguson, Consultant

"Ivan embraces a way of thinking that I am hoping spreads like wildfire across the planet, investing to the benefit of all. I have seen his personal investments and those of his clients result in happier communities and improved living conditions for the direct beneficiaries and for the surrounding communities. Yes, I admire Ivan greatly, and the spread of his PhilanthroInvestor concept. It benefits every single one of us."

Karen Nelson Bell, Best-Selling Author, Nothing Down for Women

"Working with Ivan has helped me fulfill my dream of being a fulltime philanthropist. My job is to spread kindness and good will every day in every way, and with Ivan's PhilanthroInvesting system, I can accomplish my financial goals and my humanitarian goals simultaneously.

"As a long-time real estate investor and trainer, I would say this is the simplest, easiest, and most efficient way for the layman to reach their own personal version of the American Dream."

Dr. Ken F. Taylor, Director of Mind-Body Medicine Clinic

"If you want to build wealth, creating a very positive cash flow, while creating strong equity and helping others, Equity & Help, Inc is perfect to work with.

"I believe Ivan, the Founder of this unique company, is a great leader who inspires and the group of people he has brought together are a force for good. Times of turmoil require creative ways to build wealth and do business, but it is also key that each one of us gives our share back to the world."

Jerry Fetta, Founder of Wealth DynamiX

"I really enjoyed reading Ivan's book. As a fellow financial educator is was refreshing to see Ivan advocating for financial literacy, personal responsibility and distinguishing between true investing and speculating. I love what Housing Philanthroinvesting stands for. Ivan has changed the game so that investing no longer has to be a "Zero Sum Game"."

Jeff Flamm, Real Estate Investor

In my mid-20s, I bought my first income property. I continued doing that over the years with great success. Ivan's book covers all the basics I have learned through trial and error. This should be a text used in every college to teach about investing. I love his approach to evaluating each investment in several ways to evaluate both risk and profitability. Investments that help other people in their life are the most rewarding investments ever. I embraced this approach after meeting Ivan and investing in Equity & Help. This book covers the principles of wise investing while being philanthropic. Every investor should read it!

Housing PhilanthroInvesting:

Invest with a Purpose

Grow your capital
while helping families own their home

Ivan Anz

Quantity sales special discounts are available on quantity purchases by corporations, associations, and others. For details, contact the publisher at the address above.

Orders by U.S. trade bookstores and wholesalers. Email info@BeyondPublishing.net

The Beyond Publishing Speakers Bureau can bring authors to your live event. For more information or to book an event contact the Beyond Publishing Speakers Bureau speak@BeyondPublishing.net

The Author can be reached directly at www.PhilanthroInvestors.com

Manufactured and printed in the United States of America distributed globally by BeyondPublishing.net

BEYOND
PUBLISHING

New York | Los Angeles | London | Sydney

ISBN Hardcover: 978-1-637922-89-7

ISBN Softcover: 978-1-63792-291-0

Legal Disclaimer

Contents

PhilanthroInvestor Defined

Philanthropist: (Merriam Webster Dictionary)

Someone who makes an active effort to promote human welfare.

Investor: (Merriam Webster Dictionary)

Someone who commits (money) in order to earn a financial return.

Someone involved or engaged, especially emotionally.

PhilanthroInvestor: (Ivan Anz)

Someone who invests money and time, engaging emotionally to promote human welfare, while earning a financial return.

Introduction

From winning to losing

The year was 2010, and I had achieved a monumental goal: Together with my family, I had successfully developed multiple businesses. The long days and late nights had paid off. The tasks that had consumed me no longer needed my daily attention, and my freed time brimmed with possibilities.

As a young man in my twenties, this should have been a moment of celebration, maybe a chance to figure out what I wanted to do with the next phase of my career. Instead, I couldn't help but feel like I hadn't done enough. Looking at images of other entrepreneurs online, I found myself lost in comparison. They drove Lamborghinis, lived in mansions, wore expensive watches, and flew private planes to lavish vacations with their families.

I craved their material possessions and their status. Maybe, if I had what those entrepreneurs had, I would finally feel accomplished, and happy.

This dream gripped me wholly. Instead of setting my sights towards building another company, I chose a different path. I wanted to become rich, fast. And there was only one way I knew how to do it: speculating in the stock and other markets.

If others could do it, so could I!

With a goal of making a million dollars, I invested 30K of my hard-earned money in Bitcoin, foreign exchange, and other stocks. I can still recall the thrill of watching my investments growing over the coming weeks. Though I couldn't see it, the experience was similar to sitting at a slot machine or card table in a casino. It was an addiction. The odds may have been stacked against me, but the pull to keep going was irresistible.

Before I knew it, managing my investments became a full-time job. I was spending just as much time trading stocks and currency as I had on my businesses as an entrepreneur. Within a short six months, my initial investment increased to a healthy $238K. The day I logged in and first saw that figure, it *almost* made it justifiable that I wasn't spending as much time with my wife. It *almost* made it excusable that I was only partially present for my life.

Almost, but not quite.

Feeling lucky and falsely justified, I started taking greater risks. I was confident that I could easily make four times as much money, so I made a large gamble with foreign exchange and stocks. This was the last one, I reasoned. Then I would be able to live the dream life I wanted, buying Louis Vuitton bags for my wife and jet-setting to tropical private beaches. All I needed was for this last piece to fall into place.

I went to sleep that night certain I would wake up to exciting news.

The next morning, when I checked my online investments, I felt sick. My robust $238K had plummeted to a mere $7K—less than the initial investment of $30K. Not only had I not made a million dollars, I had lost capital, lost time, and I had lost months of my life that could have been spent with loved ones or doing something purposeful.

The shift in my well-being was instant and extreme. I felt like nothing was in my control. I felt like I would never be able to achieve what others had.

I had failed.

Those were the darkest months of my life. I suffered from lack of sleep and stress-induced health issues. The fear and anxiety were suffocating. Doctors did the best they could to treat my symptoms, but nothing could fix the cause. I had lost our money, and there was no getting it back. The despair was crushing, and the question I now faced was: how can I start over?

An unexpected turn

That same year, while picking up the pieces of my life, something unexpected happened. In 2007 I had started a private neighborhood in Argentina, and I was still selling lots three years later. After my loss of almost $238K in one night, a couple came to me asking to see the neighborhood. Despite feeling low, I drove them to a lot that was for sale. They were kind, warm people, and I felt my spirit lift being with them.

They were instantly enamored by the lot and could imagine building a home there, their children running around the neighborhood. The kids were happy, saying, "Daddy, daddy, we want to live here!" The dad came out of the car and told me that he could not afford to buy this lot. I asked him if he could get a loan from the bank. He said he wouldn't qualify. Then I asked how much down payment he could afford. The number he shared was almost nothing because they lived paycheck to paycheck.

I remember sitting in the car with them, my eyes welling. Here were two hard working people, each with a job, and a desire to create a safe home for their family. To saddle them with the normal terms of purchasing a lot in this neighborhood would have added financial strain to their lives. And yet, it didn't seem right to turn them away from this dream, either.

How can I help them? I wondered. Suddenly, an idea came to me, and before I knew what I was doing, I said, "The lot is yours. You don't have to pay me anything for the first thirty days. Let's figure out terms that work for you to pay it off over many years."

As soon as I said the words, I knew they were right. The couple beamed. In that moment, I felt like I had made a breakthrough. I wasn't thinking about my recent failure. In fact, it seemed small compared to the swelling happiness on that lot. I would still make money through the sale, but why couldn't I help these people at the same time? What if my first priority in business was to help families get what they needed, and my second priority was to make it work financially?

I told the family there was one thing left to do. This moment felt important somehow, though I didn't know why yet. A ritual was needed for all of us—to commemorate this new, emerging chapter.

At my request, we returned to the lot on a different day and they planted a tree, something they could watch grow over the years. I asked them to meet me by the tree with their kids for a small ceremony. Beforehand, I put two torches in the ground and stretched a green ribbon across it. Together, the family cut the ribbon and crossed the threshold to their future.

The birth of PhilanthroInvesting

I've always had a passion for creating organizations that have legacy and purpose. To me, it doesn't make sense to create something that isn't resilient enough to survive for at least 100 years—100 years of changes in the economy, changes in the world, and changes in the consumer market. If an organization is truly resilient, it can surpass the challenge of an evolving planet, and serve generation after generation.

I'm not interested in accumulating power for myself. I love helping others and seeing my companies serve humanity, enabling life to flourish and expand.

It took losing my money in speculation to truly wake up to what was important. What effect does the all-consuming nature of the stock market create on an investor's mind, their health, their family, their job, and, if they're an entrepreneur, their employees? What effect does it create on humanity overall? I was no longer my best self, and I knew my ripples in the world had gone from positive to negative. If I wasn't living my purpose of uplifting humanity, not only was I impacted, but others were too.

When that family came to me, it was a lightbulb moment. I suddenly knew there was a way to grow my money and feel aligned with my values. I knew there was a way to go beyond making money for just my own benefit.

I donned my entrepreneur's hat once more and started asking new questions. What would it look like to align my investments with my purpose? How could the benefits of building one's wealth be exponential, not only improving the investor's life, but the world?

Slowly, PhilanthroInvesting was born.

What is PhilanthroInvesting?

In the chapters to come, you're going to learn all about PhilanthroInvesting—what it is, why it's an ideal investment, how it can address the world's biggest problems, and most importantly, how you can do it. This journey will show you how you can grow your capital while helping others, all while investing in something that moves the world in a positive direction.

The root words behind PhilanthroInvesting are fairly intuitive. We know that an "investor" is someone who invests their money in order to make a profit. The word "philanthropy" comes from the Greek *philanthrōpía*, meaning a "love for mankind." It is defined as an altruistic concern for human welfare and advancement, usually manifested through the donation of money, property, or work to a meaningful cause.

Albert Einstein once stated, "Only a life lived for others is a life worthwhile."

You don't have to be a genius, a wealthy business owner, or a celebrity to be a philanthropist. It is not relative to what you have, but what you give.

For example, if a rich man gave $100 to a charity, that could be considered a gesture. If a poor man gave away $10 to someone in need, he could be considered a philanthropist.

I have always enjoyed being around those who are providing help. My parents raised me in an environment of "give it back and pay it forward." When I was a twelve-year-old growing up in Argentina, my parents owned a car dealership. Their small company grew, and as they achieved success, they found more opportunities to give back.

When she wasn't working the family business, my mom was busy serving as the president of the Rotary Club. Every August, when we celebrated the Day of the Children, my parents purchased hundreds of children's toys and gave them away. On more than one occasion, I witnessed my parents gift a car to a priest in our church, to charity, or to one of their employees. They set an example for me. They were giving, and they were making a difference. I watched their dealership become the number one in their network in our state!

Watching the faces of children receiving toys, or a deserving employee receiving a surprise car, I saw the joy that giving to others brought my parents. There was something magical about experiencing this all firsthand.

Philanthropy is not just a word; it is an intent followed by an action, and it creates a meaningful impact.

Now, let's put the two concepts together: A PhilanthroInvestor is someone who invests money and time, engaging emotionally to promote human welfare while earning a financial return.

PhilanthroInvesting is a new level of consciousness that embodies doing things with this spirit of giving back. I believe that, in the future, investors will increasingly feel a responsibility to use their investments to create the world they want for future generations. I created PhilanthroInvesting as a model and a practice for those who are ready to go beyond making money for the sake of money; they want to make money to create a better life, for themselves and others.

If that mission excites you, then you're going to love this book.

PhilanthroInvesting is key to creating a better world

Investing is a powerful tool. There are trillions of dollars in the stock market. That money, to some degree, influences how our world operates, and the kinds of lives people lead.

Any yet there is a lot of confusion about the investing world.

7

What do the terms mean? How do you actually build wealth? How do you know where to invest your money, and how much to put in? Should you hire someone to help, or do it yourself? What do you need to know to be successful?

Moreover, do you know what kind of world your current investments are creating?

Today, our world faces myriad challenges. Only 8% of the global population lives in environments with good air quality. More people die from unsafe drinking water than from war. Billions of families worldwide will never own their homes. Almost a billion people do not have access to electricity worldwide, and even more are illiterate.

The animal population has declined nearly 70% in fifty years, and 1.5 million animals are euthanized every year in the U.S. alone. Over 95% of the world's population experiences health problems, and yet the issues are varied, as more than one billion humans suffer from hunger, and others die from obesity and the impacts of eating highly processed foods.

These statistics are only a glimpse of the world in 2020, and a very small one at that. Our crises are vast. As the Earth's population grows and our planet deteriorates, most of these conditions worsen.

As an entrepreneur, I like to imagine what's possible. When I consider these statistics, I see that our planet can be reimagined and reorganized to a far greater ideal. On this ideal Earth, every family has their own home, individuals eat organic and pure food, and animals and humans drink pure water and breathe pure air. I see a world where millions of lives are protected from structural damage brought on by poorly built homes and buildings; a world where every functional space creates and renews its own energy; a world without illiteracy.

It's a world of wellness over disease, where artistic talent is recognized and developed, and where investors enjoy true financial freedom through purpose, knowledge, control, engagement, and fulfillment.

Right now, more than 450 billion dollars are gambled worldwide, and 90% of people lose money in the stock market. When I consider those numbers, I see a path forward to create a new kind of investment that redistributes money away from speculation, while also contributing to a better future. I don't want anyone to experience the stomach-plummeting feeling I had when I lost tens of thousands of dollars overnight, for no reason other than personal accumulation. Instead, I want them to feel empowered and emboldened to grow their wealth in a reliable, exciting way, all while helping improve life on Earth.

The PhilanthroInvesting series

This book is one in a series, each exploring a challenge facing our modern world, and how PhilanthroInvesting can address it. The book you hold in your hands focuses on the housing crisis.

Although the U.S. is one of the richest countries in the world and controls one of the most powerful currencies on the planet, over 50% of the population does not qualify for a traditional mortgage from a bank. As a result, this means that more than 50% of the population will never own their home, or experience the stability and the pride of homeownership.

There is not a shortage of homes; there is an accessibility issue, and an issue with how we approach traditional investing. Fortunately, these issues can be addressed.

Homeownership is an important part of a healthy family and a healthy society. It's easy to think that a stable home life only affects the individuals involved, but that's not the case. Homeownership affects the well-being of society at large, including you!

The mission of my book series is to increase the consciousness level of the investment world, which will result in fewer people suffering from speculative investments, and more people liberated to invest with a purpose. We are going to take a deeper look at the housing crisis and how you can implement the PhilanthroInvesting model to make a difference to your bottom line and the world. Or, as I like to say, we're going to divert money from Wall Street to Your Street.

What you will learn

This book has dual functionality. Just as the name PhilanthroInvesting suggests, it's part investing, part philanthropy. In this book, I want to take you out of confusion about the world of investing, and show you how you can help impact the global housing crisis through PhilanthroInvesting.

By the end, you will understand the basics of investing, how to identify an ideal investment, why PhilanthroInvesting is the only path to true financial freedom, how PhilanthroInvesting can solve the housing crisis, and finally, how to become a Housing PhilanthroInvestor in eight steps.

To support this process, at the end of each chapter is a series of questions to help you reflect on the concepts of PhilanthroInvesting and the world you want to create. I've also included a glossary of terms at the back of the book. If you don't know a term, I'd encourage you to flip to the back and increase your level of understanding before moving forward. This book is meant to be accessible, and, most importantly, actionable.

I would like to invite you to believe in the power of investments to improve not only your life and the lives of your family members, but also the lives of other human beings. To me, there is nothing more fulfilling than a win-win situation, and PhilanthroInvesting delivers a triple win—for Philanthro-Investors, for homeowners, and for better neighborhoods.

Are you ready? Because it's time to increase your investment literacy so you can journey beyond wealth to true financial freedom; it's time to help families who are struggling and who want the pride of homeownership.

It's time to Awaken Your PhilanthroInvestor Within and change the world's housing crisis.

Take a Moment to PhilanthroInvest

Consider the dream of having every person in the world lead with philanthropy. This can be accomplished with time and money, and involves the simple act of helping others.

If all companies gave 1%, or even 0.1%, to humanity to forward causes, how do you envision it would change the condition of the planet?

_____

_____

_____

_____

_____

Were you raised in a loving home where acts of helping and giving to others were normalized, taught, and expected? How did that shape you? If not, can you see the value in giving to others?

_____

_____

_____

_____

_____

Have you ever played in the speculative investment game? What was your experience? Did you suffer gains, losses, or both?

_____

_____

_____

_____

_____

Did you reach your investment goals, and if so, were you fulfilled?

_____

_____

_____

_____

_____

Did you find yourself wanting more, but not knowing how to achieve it?

_____

_____

_____

_____

_____

Have you considered the idea of giving in order to receive?

_____

_____

_____

_____

_____

Chapter 1
The Game of Investing

The antidote to confusion is knowledge

Before we get into the specifics about PhilanthroInvesting, it's important to take you out of confusion around investing.

One of the most powerful tools in investing is knowledge. Knowledge about the basic concepts of money and wealth; knowledge about the actions that lead to true financial freedom (and what that even is); even knowledge about how to guide the people who might be managing your money for you.

Knowledge is power. Without it, we aren't in control of our money. One of the reasons so many people lose money when investing can be traced back to a lack of knowledge. This was certainly true in my own experience.

By possessing the right knowledge about the basics of investing, you not only equip yourself to create the financial future you desire, but you can also share it with your loved ones. If you have a partner or family, and you're responsible for managing your money, what will they do if something happens to you? My goal is to make the information in this book as accessible as possible so that it can be shared widely.

In this chapter, we will define basic concepts, explore how money is a tool for getting what you want, and understand the seven most important factors in investing. But first, we must start by identifying what this game is all about in the first place.

The game of investing: which one are you playing?

I see life as an exciting, engaging game, and we have the power to choose what kind of game we play.

Do you choose the game of marriage? Of creating a family? Of pursuing a spiritual path? The game of finding your calling and developing your career?

The games we play in life are predicated on what we ultimately desire. We pursue things we want.

Like any game, there are rules, and objectives. Some games have one winner, and some have multiple winners. The best game is the one where everybody wins.

When you pursue the games you want to play in life, you are in control of these variables. However, sometimes we end up playing other people's games, and we are subjected to their rules, their objectives, and their definition of a winner or winners.

Consider the game of gambling. Gambling is the house's game (the "house" being the owners of the casino). You know how they say the house always wins? That's because they've created the rules for their games. Their objective is to make as much money as possible. The game is only "rigged" if you don't understand what you're signing up for when you put your token into the slot machine. If you think you're in charge of this game, you're going to be disappointed time and again. But if you know that the rules of the game are created to favor the house, then you go into the experience expecting to lose your money to the primary winner, and you plan to simply enjoy the ambiance or your friend's company.

Many people experience the world of investing in the same way a gambling addict experiences a casino. They don't know the rules, and they don't know the objectives of the other players. (At the casino, the house wants to make money at your expense; in the market, there are a lot of other players who also want to make money, and it's a zero-sum game.)

It is said that two primary emotions drive investors' decisions in the stock market: greed and fear. When things look good, we increase our investments out of greed. When the market is doing poorly, we become fearful and withdraw our money.

Emotional reactivity is never a useful approach when playing a game. Instead, we want to cultivate a clear, calm, cool intelligence. We have to know what game we're playing, and how to play it.

Or, perhaps, we might long for a different game altogether, one where winning doesn't happen at the expense of others but uplifts everyone involved.

A better game

I believe that we all have an inherent desire to do good. I also believe that one of the paths to healing our world is to create better games for people to play.

That is one of my primary goals with PhilanthroInvesting—to create a better game in the investment world.

Imagine having investment opportunities that align with your values, and are helpful, transparent, and purposeful. Imagine an investment game that engages you emotionally, and goes beyond using money solely to make more money. Imagine a game that improves your life and all of humanity. That's the game I want to play!

If we are to play a better game, we need to be the ones who

create it. The objective of this game is to go beyond wealth into true financial freedom, which includes characteristics like fulfillment, legacy, and enjoyment. The rules of the game are to make money while improving humanity. And we'll know when we're winning because we will feel the impact of growing our wealth and engaging in The Law of Betterment (more about that in Chapter 4).

This is a game for you, and for our world.

The choice is yours

My goal is not to be critical of the market, or how people choose to invest. Whatever game you play, I don't think the choice should be driven by external voices telling you what you "should" do. I trust every person to listen to their internal voice and make the choice that's best for them.

What I'm trying to convey is that in order to actually listen to that internal guidance, you must first start with knowledge about what you're doing. I want you to be empowered to choose the life you want, in every way, but especially with your money. You've worked hard. You've provided for yourself, and possibly your loved ones. That expenditure of energy and time deserves consideration and respect. However that manifests for you is exactly right.

I'm not here to criticize consumerism, either. There's nothing wrong with wanting a Ferrari. For some people, expensive cars are an art form. The tires, the interior, the technology—it's a passion akin to collecting art. The disconnect I see in our society is when passion becomes overconsumption. There are plenty of stories of millionaires and billionaires who are miserable. And yet they cannot stop pursuing material items, because they think it is the only path to happiness.

This all comes back to what game you're playing. If your goal is to feel fulfilled, purposeful, and happy in your life, you might find an emptiness in material items. They ultimately don't give you abiding satisfaction.

Know the games you're playing, and also know yourself. What do you actually want? If you were to reach the end of your life and look back, would you have lived in accordance with your values and purposes?

The market isn't inherently bad. It all comes down to your choice. You get to choose what the best version of yourself is, and go after that. Whatever you choose—whether helping humanity is part of your best version or not—it will dictate your actions and your behaviors. Your focus orients your life. If you focus on having a red car, *and* a blue car, *and* a white car, *and* a black car, your behaviors will orient in that direction. If you choose to help families stay in their homes so they can give promising futures to their children, your behaviors will orient in that direction.

From here on out, I will be sharing how to do the latter. But know as we move forward that the choice is always yours. You have the gift and the responsibility to choose how you want to live.

What is wealth?

Definitions are important, especially when it comes to the basics of investing. Our knowledge begins by understanding what the terms mean, and how these concepts function together.

Let's start with the most basic term: wealth.

A lot of people want wealth, but what is it? How does it operate in your life? Soon we'll be reviewing the "path to wealth." It's good to know what we're getting ourselves into!

Wealth is a plentiful supply of a particular desirable thing.

What I love about this definition is that it allows you, the wealth-builder, to determine what is "desirable." Perhaps time with your family is the most desirable thing in your life, and you organize everything else around that resource. Or perhaps the most desirable thing is sailing, and your goal is to be rich in both cash and time to sail the Atlantic.

Once more, this entire journey is about putting you in the driver's seat of your life, by giving you the knowledge to control your wealth, however you define it.

Obviously, this is a book about investing, so we're going to be talking about the tool of money—which is also a desirable thing—and how we can grow our money while creating other desirable things. Like a better world.

The archaic meaning of "wealth" is "well-being." It's a poignant connection. The more you accumulate things you truly desire, the more well-being you'll experience.

There have been many experiments that have looked at the relationship between money and happiness. What they've found is that the amount of money we have does indeed impact our happiness, but only to a certain extent. Once our basics are covered, we need something else to feel "wealthy" or to achieve "well-being." Thus, money is a tool to create well-being, but as these studies suggest, once we achieve that level of financial solvency, we need something more to feel truly wealthy.

Money is a tool

If wealth is the abundance of a desirable thing, money is one of those desirable things.

Money is something generally accepted as a medium of exchange, a measure of value, or a means of payment.

Money is an asset or something that has value. It's also a tool used to achieve a desired outcome.

An important distinction to make is that money is not exclusively cash. Cash is a form of money, but money, according to the definition above, is something that is generally accepted as a medium of exchange. Money, therefore, is any kind of asset, or thing of value. You might trade that asset for cash, or you might trade it for something else, like a piece of land or a car, both of which are forms of money. Money includes all of your wealth.

When you're referencing bills or coins in your country's currency, the proper word would be "cash" rather than "money."

In order to skillfully use the tool of money, we need to understand how money works. A hammer can be used to put nails in a wall. The hammer adds leverage to achieve an objective that would be difficult to accomplish with just your hand (ouch!). But if you don't know how to use that hammer, you might not succeed in achieving your goal—maybe you try to put the nail in backwards, or swing a hammer without paying attention, creating multiple holes in your wall. Knowing how to use a hammer will help you achieve your goal of hanging a picture.

Money is like a hammer. When you know how to wield it properly through your investments, it can give you leverage to achieve things you otherwise wouldn't be able to accomplish.

However, when handled poorly (as an "irresponsible investor"), money will choose its own path as you swing it blindly towards the wall. And it can create a lot of holes in your pocket!

Control your money; don't let your money control you.

Because this book deals with investing, I'm not going to talk about how to make money. We're going to talk about what to do with your money once it has been earned. If you're reading this book before you're ready to invest, I congratulate you on wanting to build your knowledge. Your first step, in the meantime, will be to go out into the world and continue exchanging your hard work for the asset of money. The more engagement, energy, and value you put into your act of creation, the more money you will get in return. Then, once you have money, you will know more about how to wield this tool appropriately.

Responsible investors combine money and purpose

At PhilanthroInvesting, we surveyed over 10,000 investors who made over $100,000 a year and asked what they cared about most when it came to their investments. There is a common perception that investors care about hands-free, passive income, but that's not what we found. In fact, these investors responded most favorably to two descriptions:

1. Investments with a purpose

2. Clear investments with clear results

It was inspiring to see so many investors elevate these qualities, and it confirmed my suspicion that people want to do good. They just need to be presented with transparent opportunities.

We need to change how we see money. Money, or cash, is

most useful when it has purpose behind it.

An irresponsible investor has a lifeless relationship with money. They have no knowledge about investing. Instead, they want to passively hand their money to someone else to manage, and they want to be given their returns, without involvement. And if they lose money, they have someone else to blame.

As I said before, if this is someone's choice, I respect that. But I'm creating a new option for the people who find this path lacking. A responsible investor, on the other hand, has a purpose behind their money. To me, a life of value is nothing more than finding a purpose that enhances humanity and inspires you, and following it every single day.

I define purpose as the reason you do something. And there are two components: a goal, and a path to get there.

Imagine a line from where you're sitting to some place in the distance. That destination is your goal. It contains a result you want to achieve. The line is a path you can walk to arrive at that destination. It's only big enough to fit you. Step by step, you move along the line. The more knowledge you gain, and the more energy you put into your engagement, the faster you'll be able to traverse this path.

Now imagine that line is as wide as a road. It's big enough for your family to join you, and some of your community members. You're taking them along your road towards an end destination, which is your goal. Along the way, the lives of everyone involved improve.

What if that line were a six-lane highway? How many people could you take along this journey? How many lives would be changed as you move towards your goal?

I call this path a Purpose Line. We're all responsible for determining the size of ours, and how quickly we want to traverse it.

Purpose is embedded in how you live, in every moment. It is something you do, not something you have. Right now, you are walking along a Purpose Line of a certain size towards the things you want. You probably have a reason behind that purpose. Maybe it's something you're really passionate about. Or maybe your current Purpose Line isn't something you chose for yourself but was chosen by someone else. If it does not fit how you want to live, you need to wake up and take control of your life again.

The ultimate goal is an outcome you'd like to see in the world, like eliminating the housing crisis, or saving the planet's water, or eradicating illiteracy. You'll know when you've arrived because everyone in the world will have a stable home, or the planet's water will be pure, or everyone will be able to read. Your purpose requires you to accumulate knowledge and tools to engage with that journey. Money is one of those tools. When we align our money with a purpose, we will be able to swing our hammer with greater efficiency, producing more powerful results.

The irresponsible investor walks in a circle of self-generated wealth that may increase or decrease, without them caring much. The responsible investor cares about the effect their money creates, finds their passion, and the reason behind why they do what they do. Then, they figure out how to expand that road, taking as many people as possible with them towards a better life.

The responsible investor invests with a purpose.

What is an investor?

Let's continue to build our knowledge by truly understanding what investing is, the basic terms, and the tools that will help you be successful.

Here's how I like to define an investor:

An investor is someone who uses their money and emotional engagement with the expectation of making a profit.

The word "invest" has interesting roots. It comes from the Latin word *vestis*, which means "clothing." So investing has its origins in protecting your body from the natural elements through clothing. It entails privacy and the basic fulfillment of a need.

Investing, at its heart, is a desire for protection. We want to prepare for a better tomorrow; we want to protect our family's well-being; we want to protect the money we've earned. Sure, some investors might take risks. Everyone's tolerance is different. And yet, that primary essence remains in investors today: beneath it all, we simply want to clothe and provide for ourselves and our loved ones.

An accumulation of losses

It can be difficult to succeed in protecting yourself and your loved ones when you don't feel in control of your investments.

There are two ways to have control. The first is you personally control how particles in this world move. For example, if I move my hand through space, I'm enacting control over that particle. The other way to have control is through someone else. I can tell my wife to move my hand through space for me.

The latter is how executives operate. They hire others to manage particles in their business or divisions; they guide others

25

to work on their behalf. Another example is you can build your house yourself, controlling the process through your own labor, or you can be the project manager and hire contractors, guiding them on how to build your house.

When it comes to investments, you can manage your own money, or you can hire someone else to do it for you. But for many people, no matter which route they pick, they still don't feel in control.

According to the Google Books Ngram Viewer, the word "investing" started to surge in usage in the 1960s, and rose exponentially until about 2004. Since then, its usage has had a downward trend. The word "investment" also has a recent downward trend, starting in the 1990s.

Use of the word "investing"

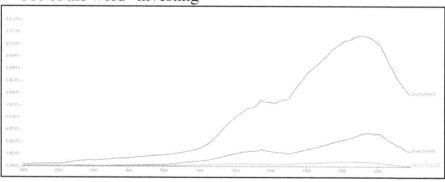

Use of the word "investment"

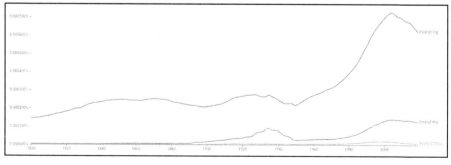

I wondered why this was. Especially in our age of greater financial literacy, global accumulation of wealth, plentiful wealth management businesses, and the proliferation of online investments through the Internet, why would these terms be less popular over the last few decades?

What I perceive, and what I will share in the next chapter in greater depth, is the vast accumulation of losses people experience in the stock or other speculative market. It's human nature to not want to relate to or talk about losses, whether it's the loss of a job, a family member, or money. If estimates are right, and 90% of investors lose money in the stock market, that to me illuminates an enormous accumulation of lost wealth. Of course, people don't want to be talking about that!

Engagement is key

Do you know where I think most people are going wrong? It's in the latter half of my definition of an investor—"…uses their *emotional engagement* with the expectation of making a profit." Part of the reason I believe we feel out of control is because we aren't actually engaging with our investments. We're merely expecting them to deliver without effort or input.

When it comes to living our purpose, actions speak louder than words. We might *say* that we care about a certain thing, but if we don't demonstrate it with our actions—including our time, and our emotional engagement—then we aren't actually making progress on our Purpose Line.

I might be so bold to say that if you don't believe in a purpose—if it doesn't increase your emotional engagement in something meaningful to you—you won't be able to control that investment. If, however, you begin engaging with your purpose, and you start learning more about it, meeting others who are involved, spending more time dedicated to it…there will be a fire lit in you. Your knowledge will expand. And your control over your investment will expand because you're taking the game into your own hands.

Investing is future-oriented

Consumerism is rooted in the present moment. There's something that we want, so we exchange cash for that item. Now we own it. The whole consumer industry is built on present-moment desires—things you want now, and your willingness to exchange an asset for them.

Investing is different. Investing has nothing to do with now and everything to do with the future. Your intention is to grow your money for a better future for yourself, for your family, for your community, and for your world. That future will eventuate, someday. But it *won't* eventuate if we only prioritize our needs in the present moment.

Let's use the example of buying a table. You've been wanting a new table for your dining room. The current one was inherited from your parents. It's a wooden table, and full of scars, pot marks, and scribbles from when your children were young. You want to buy a new table made of glass, with intricately shaped metal legs. There's one online that you really like, and you're getting ready to purchase it.

What does that table cost? It will obviously be listed for an amount that you will pay, but what other costs are involved?

Not only are you buying a table with that money, you're also spending part of your future. If that money had been put towards an investment, and it had gained compounding interest over the next ten years, what kind of future could it have contributed to, for yourself and others?

Every purchase you make in the present moment takes away from future opportunities. And when you lose money in your investments, you not only lose opportunities in the present but also your future.

Now, as we consider this, it's important to tell you that we need to strike a balance. The future is important, but so is something else: *enjoyment*!

If you aren't enjoying your life right now, what's the point? Our money is merely a tool that can provide both an enjoyable present and an enjoyable future. However, you choose to strike that balance is completely up to you. If the dining room table is within your budget and it will bring you long-term joy, buy it! Ideally, you want to buy things you will enjoy in the present moment with income from your investments. The income you make earning a living then goes towards expanding your investments.

Keep in mind that our enjoyment expands when we positively impact others. (Again, more on this in The Law of Betterment, Chapter 4.) The more we give others, the more exponential our present-moment enjoyment will be.

The seven factors of investing

In order to truly understand the game of investing, we must first know the basic rules. I'm using "rules" broadly here to mean "how investing works." When learning chess, you're told the names of each piece, how they move, and how you win. These variables create a foundation for you to be proficient at chess.

In investing, there are seven primary factors or pieces on the board:

- Assets
- Liabilities
- Profits
- Cash flow
- Taxes
- Investor "hats"
- Investment management tools for responsible investing

These factors are unavoidable truths. They exist in the game of investing whether we want them to or not. The more we learn about them, the more control we have when investing.

1. Assets

An asset is, in the broadest sense of the term, **a useful or valuable thing.**

Just as there are many kinds of valuable things, there are many kinds of assets. What is considered an "asset" might change over time, depending on what's valuable to the market.

Some examples of assets are: real estate, a business, precious metals, classic cars, cash, land, intellectual property, bonds, stocks, gemstones, fine art, construction equipment, web domains, cryptocurrency...the list goes on!

In the context of investing, an asset is **anything that can be owned or controlled to produce value, and could produce positive economic value**. This is important. Ideally, your asset, whatever it might be, will appreciate in value over time, or generate profit in some way ("profit" defined below).

How do you ensure your asset doesn't lose value? By

engaging yourself in the investment of this asset until it creates capital growth and cash flow (both also defined below).

One final word on assets: the term comes from Old French *asez*, which means "enough." Once again, this model of investing can be personalized to suit your needs. What is "enough" in the context of your life? For some people, it is enough to live in a tiny house in the middle of the mountains, where they can bike to the store with their family. For someone else, "enough" means a large house near the city, with the ability to eat at fancy restaurants three nights a week. And for others, "enough" means being able to contribute positively to the world.

Spend some time considering your current assets, and what your goals are for those assets. When will you know you've won the game, and you have "enough"?

2. Profits

Profit can be defined as: A financial gain, especially the difference between the amount earned and the amount spent in buying, operating, or producing an asset.

Let's say you have a side business knitting hats and sweaters. You sell them in person at a local market. Your expenses to produce these items include the cost of yarn and knitting needles, the amount of gas it takes to get to the market, and miscellaneous additions, like buttons or sew-on labels. When you set the price for your hats and sweaters, it includes: 1. the amount spent when producing your goods, 2. the time it took, and 3. the profit you want to earn on top of that. If you spent $10/sweater, and you charge $25, your profit is $15 dollars ($25-$10 = $15).

$100,000 Bank loan
+ $120,000 Bank's interest ← Bank's profit
(4% = $4,000 x 30 years)
_____
= Total Financial Commitment

Just as there are different kinds of assets, there are different kinds of profits, depending on how you're investing your money. For example, when a bank lends money, it earns profit through interest payments. If a family receives a loan from a bank for $100,000 to buy a house, and they pay 4% interest over thirty years, each monthly payment will go towards two things: the initial loan amount (called the "principal") and the interest rate. The interest is how the bank makes money. That is their profit.

The word profit comes from the Latin word for "progress" (*profectus*) or "to advance" (*proficere*). I love this connection. The more valuable your asset, the more profit it will produce, the more your wealth will advance, and the greater your opportunity to make progress in your purpose!

3. Liabilities

A liability is **a thing for which someone is responsible, especially a debt or financial obligation.** The term "liable" can also be thought of as "responsible." We are responsible for every asset we own, and almost every asset has a liability attached to it. If you own a classic car, that car can crash. If you own a business, that business can go bankrupt. If an asset's value is directly related to external variables—like market fluctuations, or the value of a currency, or the preservation of a physical thing— it has the potential to one day lose value. Every asset has inherent liability.

In order to protect yourself against the liabilities of your assets, there are different kinds of insurance. You can protect your car, your art, and your home with insurance. When we explore Housing PhilanthroInvesting, we'll discuss how to legally separate yourself from your asset, so that you cannot be held liable should something go wrong.

Any debts you have are also a liability. This includes credit card debt, loans, or money owed to a friend. When we talk about your net worth in the four tools of investing, you will see how debts impact your overall wealth.

There are many financial gurus who teach that you must take on greater liability by going into debt in order to make money. I don't believe that. I believe in growing wealth organically. Here's why: the attention you use to control your debt can instead be used to create more profits. Put that same attention towards growing what you have, and making more money, rather than increasing your liabilities through debt. True financial freedom, as we will discuss in Chapter 3, includes the state of being debt-free. It is a state of having total financial independence.

Two ways to organically grow your assets without going into debt are:

1. Use your own creativity through entrepreneurship to generate more assets, and then invest those assets for greater growth. A human being generates what he wishes because he or she gives it attention and engagement. Shift your engagement to what you truly want.

2. Find an equity partnership. If you identify an asset you want

to invest in, but you don't have the money, find an equity partner who can invest with you. You will own less of the asset, but you can work with this person so that you both benefit, and, if you PhilanthroInvest, the world benefits at the same time. You see? You expanded your Purpose Line by inviting a partner that likes to live the same purpose.

4. Cash flow

Cash is a type of asset and is the one that flows the most. It is essentially as the words imply: **cash that flows to you from your investment activities**. If you trade an asset—like a house—for cash, the cash that flows to you is your cash flow.

There are three kinds of cash flow: capital cash flow, profit cash flow, and liability cash flow.

Capital cash flow is the money that flows back to you equal to your original investment. If you spent $100,000 on a house, and you sell it for $120,000, $100,000 of that money is your capital cash flow.

Any improvements you made to the house are also part of what you spent on this asset and are capital cash flow. If you re-tiled the bathroom and built a deck for a total of $10,000, and you sold the house for $120,000, now your capital cash flow is $110,000 (the original purchase amount of $100,000 + $10,000 for improvements). When you make an investment, you definitely want to recuperate your original cash. But you also want to go beyond that!

HOUSE SOLD FOR: $120,000
HOUSE PURCHASED FOR: − $100,000 *capital cash flow*
IMPROVEMENTS COSTS: − $10,000 *capital cash flow*
————————————————————————————
        FINANCIAL GAIN = $10,000 *profit cash flow*

Profit cash flow is the amount of cash that flows back to you above your original investment. In the first example, when the house sold for $120,000, your profit cash flow is $20,000. If you invest $10,000 for improvements and sell for $120,000, now your profit cash flow is $10,000 ($120,000 − $110,000). This is your financial gain from the investment. The greater the profit cash flow, the better. Investors often reinvest their profit cash flow in order to further grow their wealth. If there's a loss of the original capital cash, that investment was undesirable.

The final type of cash flow is liability cash flow. When you exchange your asset for cash, any amount that belongs to someone else is liability cash flow. This includes a loan from a bank, a loan from a friend, or any other entity that gave you money to acquire this asset. If you take a loan from a bank, not only is that principal amount part of your liability cash flow, but also the interest the bank makes. Liability cash flow can grow over time because of interest payments. This is one of the reasons why I don't believe you should go into debt for your investments. You want to maximize your profit cash flow and minimize your liability cash flow.

An asset is valuable when it generates profit cash flow. Profit cash flow can grow exponentially if you reinvest it, and generate

35

even more profit cash flow. This is the power of compounding interest, which we'll get into below.

5. Taxes

Taxes are a reality in every country. Depending on where you live, the rules will be unique to that location. In almost every country in the world, investments have the potential for tax benefits. You can likely save money on your taxes through your investments.

This might seem like tedious knowledge, but it's important to know. Tax codes are another tool. Just as the "money hammer" can achieve great things when used appropriately, taxes are like another useful tool: a saw. They can cut off pieces of wood, just as investments can reduce your taxes!

Learn about the tax laws in your country, and don't hesitate to spend money on a good accountant. They will also know the tax codes intimately, and it will be their legal duty to represent your interests and save money where possible. They will help you optimize the value of your investments.

6. Investor hats

Although we use the word "invest" broadly, there are different ways to invest your money. I call these the "investor hats." Just like a collection of hats in your closet, the investor hats are at your disposal and can be worn and removed at will.

The six investor hats are:

- Lender
- Leaser
- Trader
- Holder

- Enhancer
- Entrepreneur

Depending on what hat you're wearing, the act of investing will look different, and how you make money will look different. A lender lends money like a bank, and they make their profit through interest payments. A trader exchanges one asset for another, with the hopes that the new asset is more valuable than the former at that point in time.

In Chapter 3 we will explore each of these hats, including their characteristics, how to optimize profit cash flow, and examples. For now, it's enough to know that these hats are part of the game of investing. The more knowledge we gain about them, the more likely we are to succeed.

7. Investment management tools for responsible investing

The last factor of investing is slightly different than the others. Whereas the previous factors are unavoidable truths, these investment management tools are things we can choose to use or not. They have the power to dramatically increase our wealth creation. I would highly recommend incorporating them on your path to wealth!

Tool #1: TIME—If it's important, schedule it

If something is important in your life, you want to give it time. If you care about improving your health, you will set aside time to cook healthy meals, move your body, and get good sleep. The more attention you give to your healthy choices, the more likely you are to progress in your goals.

Or, if you care about helping your kids with their homework, you schedule it in your calendar. Then, every evening from 5 to 6 p.m., you sit with them at the kitchen table and help solve math problems.

We schedule what we care about. We give it our time and attention. The same is true for our wealth. If wealth is important to you, you should schedule it!

What do I mean by that? Well, you should schedule two kinds of meetings to review your wealth progress: a weekly meeting, and a monthly meeting.

During each monthly meeting, you will review your investments (which is the second tool) and make a plan going forward (which is the third tool). How are your investments doing? Do you want to make any changes? If so, when is your deadline? Spend at least an hour diving into the particulars and

taking inventory. This meeting is part of emotionally engaging with your investments, and controlling the particles.

The weekly meeting is a brief check-in with last month's plan—are you making progress towards your goals? What else do you need to do so that, during your next monthly meeting, you'll feel accomplished?

Prioritize your wealth by scheduling it.

I would also like to add that it's useful to schedule the monthly meeting with someone else. Whether it's your life partner, a mentor, or a friend, find someone who can be a sounding board. Share your objectives with them, and review your investments together to see how well they match what you're trying to accomplish. This person serves as an accountability partner and someone who can provide feedback or ideas if your investments need adjusting.

If you are married or have a partner, it is important for them to join these conversations with you. You might be the primary driver of your investments, but they need to understand how your wealth is building. That way, if something were to happen to you, they would be prepared to take over.

Tool #2: DATA—Analyze the evolution of your investor data

In your monthly meetings, there are four calculations you want to do in order to truly understand your current wealth status. The first one is called your net worth.

Net worth

To calculate, you're going to need two numbers: your total assets, and your total liabilities.

Net worth = Assets – Liabilities

Remember, your assets are "useful and valuable things," and can range from cash, to real estate, to classic cars, to other valuable items in which you have invested. I would recommend having a system for tracking your assets, as well as your liabilities, like a spreadsheet.

Your net worth is a snapshot of your wealth at any moment. It is constantly fluctuating depending on the value of your assets and liabilities. When you calculate your net worth, you're capturing a moment in time.

For example, if my total assets are $750,000 and my total liabilities are $100,000, then my net worth is $650,000 ($750,000 – $100,000). Now let's say, in the next moment, my investments grow by $8,000. My net worth is now $658,000 (758,000 – $100,000).

You increase your net worth by growing your assets and shrinking your liabilities. You can grow your assets by trading profit earned for more assets, with the anticipation that they will generate even more profit cash flow. This is the strategy for abundantly growing your wealth. Once you gather this data at each monthly meeting, you will use it to make a plan about what to do next, if anything (which is the next step).

I'd like to make another note about net worth: I love how simple the equation is because there's no mystery about how you increase your net worth. You either increase your assets, or you decrease your liabilities. One easy and fast way to increase your assets right now is to reflect on your lifestyle.

	January	February	March
Assets	$500,000	$600,000	$650,000
Liabilities	-$430,000	-$390,000	-$390,000
Net Worth	$70,000	$210,000	$260,000

Your money is an asset. The more you save and put towards investments, the greater your net worth will be. This means that the less you spend on your lifestyle, the more money you have for growing wealth.

Warren Buffet, acclaimed billionaire investor, still lives in the same Nebraska home he bought in 1958 for $31,500! He could obviously afford a much more expensive home, but he chooses to invest that money in other ways. Similarly, Jeff Bezos, founder of Amazon, drove an old 1996 Honda Accord even after he became a billionaire.

By maintaining a level of lifestyle, both Buffet and Bezos were able to grow their assets much faster than if they were to develop expensive habits as their money increased. They put more attention on their investor hats than on their consumption, which made a difference in their wealth.

This principle will be important in Chapter 3 when we talk about the path to wealth. This principle is also why our weekly meetings are important. If we aren't paying attention, our lifestyle habits can grow without us noticing, negatively impacting our net worth. We're always working to strike a balance between enjoying life now and investing in the future we want. Imagine if you dedicated the same time to your wealth journey as you did to looking at clothing, cars, or houses online! Our spending habits are aligned with our values, which is reflected in our net worth, and how we spend our time.

The next three calculations—return on investment (ROI), cash on cash return, and capital rate—are ways to assess the performance of your current investments. These calculations are useful if you're deciding whether or not to sell an investment. All three are portrayed as percentages.

Return on investment

Return on investment (ROI) is a performance metric used to evaluate the return on an investment related to the cost of that investment.

ROI = (Current value of investment − Cost of investment) ÷ Cost of investment

$$ROI = \frac{\overset{(current\ value)}{\$250{,}000} - \overset{(cost\ of\ investment)}{\$200{,}000}}{\underset{(cost\ of\ investment)}{\$200{,}000}} = \frac{\$50{,}000}{\$200{,}000} = 0.25 = 25\%$$

If I spent $200,000 to purchase a home, and the value of the home right now based on the market is $250,000, my ROI would be 25% ((250,000 − 200000) ÷ 200000 = .25).

The ROI of your investments will change based on the current valuation, which is why I recommend calculating it every month at your finances meeting to understand the evolution of your investor data.

Cash on cash return and capital rate of return

These two percentages depict the percentage of cash flow that's coming back to you from an investment. But they're slightly different—the cash on cash will tell you your return based on your original investment; the capital rate (or cap rate) will tell you your return based on its value in the market right now (which is useful if you're considering selling).

Cash on cash return = Annual pretax cash flow ÷ Total cash invested

Capital rate of return = Net operating income ÷ Current market value of asset

By doing all four of these calculations—net worth, ROI, cash on cash return, and cap rate—you will gain a comprehensive picture of your portfolio each month. Then you can use this information to make a plan.

Tool #3: Make a plan

At the end of each monthly meeting, create a plan. Which of your investments performed the worst? Which performed the best? Are your investments currently aligned with your values? Are they contributing to a better world? Do they reflect your purpose? Is your net worth growing? What actions do you need to take this month to improve your overall net worth in the direction of true financial freedom?

Revisit the numbers next month and ask yourself these questions again. If your net worth is improving month after month, don't make major changes. Reinforce behaviors that increase your net worth, and correct the behaviors that decrease it. If your net worth is worsening, work with your wealth partner to determine what needs to change. Do you need to shift your investments? Do you need to reduce your liabilities? Use the knowledge you gain in this book to brainstorm the right path forward.

Create a target goal for your net worth, then work backwards to construct a plan for getting there. Review your progress every week between your monthly meetings. (Remember, if it's important, schedule it! I would recommend setting aside thirty minutes to one hour for your weekly check-ins.)

It might be that you have someone who manages your investments for you. This is a great way to work with a professional and feel confident about how your money is being handled. However, it's very important that you do not treat financial management as a passive relationship. If you aren't knowledgeable about investments, then you won't be able to manage your manager. Remember, it's *your* wealth, nobody else's, and you're responsible for it.

Every executive delegates, but they can only delegate effectively if they know what they're asking someone else to do, and if they can truly guide the process. You need to be able to work with your manager so that they align your investments with your purpose. Establish boundaries. How comfortable are you with risk-taking? Are you only willing to lose ten percent of your money? Twenty? Ideally zero! You are responsible for creating parameters with your manager, otherwise, they will make decisions based on their own guidance, rather than yours. If you feel like you don't have enough knowledge to make a decision, ask someone, or conduct research. There is no shame in reaching out to someone who's knowledgeable and asking a question to increase your knowledge.

Even if your money is being managed, I would still suggest having a meeting at least once a month wherein you review your investments. You want to know how things are going so that you can ensure your manager is truly advancing you along the path to wealth!

Tool #4: Compound interest

Compound interest—sometimes called compounding interest—is a powerful tool. It can be thought of as earning interest on interest.

If you invest $1,000 and earn 10% interest annually, the second year you will have $1,100. The next year, you won't earn another $100…instead, you will earn 10% of the new total of $1,100, which is $110. Your total investment is now $1,210.

That same investment of $1,000—without any money added, and with the same interest rate—would grow to $17,449.40 in twenty years, all because of the power of compound interest, which earned you an additional $16,449.40!

As you can see, with compound interest, you continue making money on your original investment, and you also start making money on interest accrued each year.

This is why it's important to balance your current lifestyle with your desired future. When you remove money from your investments, not only do you withdraw that single amount, but you also miss all of the compound interest that money would have made over the years.

To leverage the tool of compound interest, use the profit cash flow from an investment to generate even more profit. This can be done one of two ways: either by keeping the investment where it is, allowing the interest to grow over the years, or by withdrawing your profit cash flow and exchanging it for a different asset that will also grow. Either way, you're continuing to circulate your wealth, allowing it to grow on itself thanks to the power of compound interest.

Compound interest is another reason to hire a good accountant when doing your taxes. Some countries have tax benefits for compound interest, or when reinvesting your profit cash flow. Your accountant will know what's possible where you live, and they will help you keep as much of your compound interest as possible!

Basics of investing, in summary

Hopefully, this information has helped you gain foundational knowledge about the basics of investing. It is impossible to succeed at a game if we don't understand the rules or objectives.

In the next chapter, we are going to use this groundwork and take a critical lens to the modern investing world. What are the primary challenges? How are people currently investing their money? And why are they losing money?

Take a Moment to PhilanthroInvest

What has been the primary source of your investing knowledge? What have you learned so far in this book that surprised you, or gave you a new perspective on investing?

_____

_____

_____

_____

_____

If you were to create a new game of investing, what would you want to change? What would the rules be? How would you know when you had won?

_____

_____

_____

_____

_____

What do you want to accomplish by investing your money?

_____

_____

_____

_____

Wealth is a plentiful supply of a particularly desirable thing. In what ways do you already feel wealthy in your life?

_____

_____

_____

_____

A Purpose Line is the path you walk to contribute to the world and achieve your goals. Are you currently living in alignment with your purpose? If so, what does that look like? If not, are you living by someone else's idea of your purpose? How would you like to change that?

_____

_____

_____

_____

Are you emotionally engaged with your current investments? How could you increase that engagement?

_____

_____

_____

_____

What important things in your life do you schedule? Do you see the benefit of scheduling monthly and weekly wealth meetings?

_____

_____

_____

_____

_____

What kind of future do you want to create through your investments?

_____

_____

_____

_____

_____

Chapter 2
The Challenges of Traditional Investing

We defined an investor as someone who uses their money and emotional engagement with the expectation of making a profit. This is a fairly broad definition. There are many ways in which you could use your money and engage emotionally with the possibility of making a profit.

When it comes to traditional investments, this might include investing in bonds, stocks, foreign exchange, or intellectual property. Someone could partake in speculation moderately or through day trading.

In order to create a new game outside the traditional world of investing, we have to understand the current system. Philanthro-Investing gives investors a new way to grow their wealth while making a positive impact on the world, but what's wrong with the current model? Why would investors want to switch away from traditional investing?

In this chapter, we're going to explore the basics of traditional investing, the primary challenges of investing, and why speculation is not the solution to these challenges, setting the premise for how PhilanthroInvesting is a true game-changer.

Life essentials

Have you ever wondered how to invest in a reliable way that doesn't involve speculation? The answer is simple: Life Essentials Investing.

When you invest in things that support basic life essentials, you add value to the world. You also know these items will always be needed. They are necessary to human survival, and they support us all in achieving our Purpose Line. By deepening your knowledge in life essentials, you avoid the risk of speculation and give life.

The ten life essentials, in order of importance, are:

1. Air
2. Water
3. Food
4. Housing
5. Clothing
6. Energy
7. Wellness
8. Education
9. Interaction with nature
10. Expression through art

If you study the history of planet Earth and humanity, you will discover that these essentials have always existed, and have always been needed. When your investments are backed by any of the above assets, you can trust that you're far away from speculation, and investing in things that, historically, have always been necessary.

Now, let's explore some of the investment vehicles you should be aware of.

The basics of stocks

The New York Stock Exchange (NYSE) is the world's largest stock exchange, with $30.1 trillion circulating as of February 2018 across thousands of companies. However, there are stock exchanges all around the world, serving as platforms for buyers and sellers to trade shares of stock in companies. Stocks equate ownership in that company.

The prices of stocks fluctuate based on many variables, including demand, market prices, company performance, and more.

Behind the paper asset of a stock is the asset that the company is bringing to humanity. For example, if you buy stock in a solar company, you own part of a company that creates clean energy. If you buy stock in an oil refinery, you own shares of a company that extracts oil from the earth. Though stocks can feel disembodied and solely numerical, they are always impacting humanity in some form or fashion based on the actions of that company.

When you own a stock, you wear one of two types of investor hats: the holder hat (when you're holding a stock), or the trader hat (when you're trading that stock for another asset).

One primary characteristic of the stock market is that it is the most difficult to predict. Think about it: if it could easily be predicted, every stock investor would be rich! The stock market, in each moment, is unpredictable. But when a company is backed by a life essential, has a good quality product and brand, and is run by a good management team, the investment is more likely to give you profit cash flow over the long term, and increase your net worth. A lot of research needs to be done to ensure an investment meets these criteria.

The basics of bonds

Bonds are ways of giving companies, organizations, or even countries money through a loan. Bonds are typically long-term investments with low interest rates. They are seen as more secure investments than stocks. That company, organization, or country becomes indebted to you.

A bond is an asset that can be transferred. The basic hat here is that of the lender. You can use the holder hat and continue holding the asset and collecting bond interest payments, or you can wear the trader hat and trade that bond (or loan it) to someone else for a profit. Of course, you would only want to trade that asset if it has increased in the market, likely due to improvements that entity has made (whether it's a company or country behind the value of the asset).

There are three basic types of bonds: A government bond, a corporate bond, and a green corporate bond.

1. A government bond: All countries need money to operate. When you buy a government bond, you are helping that country achieve its goals, and they will be financially indebted to you.

2. A corporate bond: For people who don't want the risk of the stock market, they can buy corporate bonds from a company they trust. Through this legal instrument, that company now owes you money. Some of them give you the option to convert the bond to stock at any time. You'll want to acquire the right knowledge through research to know when it is advantageous to trade the bond for stocks.

3. A green corporate bond: This is a bond that specifically supports a company with a social impact purpose. The company has some sort of mission to improve humanity.

One of the main differences between a bond and a stock is a stock market investment makes you a partial owner of that company, whereas a bond is merely money lent to the company.

The basics of intellectual property

Perhaps a less common asset, but one I'd like to briefly cover, is intellectual property (IP). IP is a valuable idea you have that is converted into functional knowledge.

IP is created by wearing the entrepreneur hat. Instead of starting a company as an asset, the idea is the asset.

For example, a book or a trademarked brand is intellectual property. The thoughts, ideas, and methodologies you are acquiring by reading this book were generated, discovered, and/or organized by me and transferred on paper in these words, so I own them. Or, if someone invents a unique methodology for cleaning windows or a new formula for glue, that could become their IP.

Intellectual property has commercial value. An entrepreneur considers an area of humanity and works to understand what would be valuable to that population. They then create an idea-based solution that can be turned into an asset.

In order to create a piece of IP, you must work with a lawyer to officially protect your idea. Every country's process is different.

Speculation

Stocks, bonds, and IP are all assets. Speculation is a type of investing behavior.

Speculation refers to the act of conducting a financial transaction that has a substantial risk of losing value, but also holds the expectation of a significant gain. People can speculate on all sorts of industries like commodities and goods, stocks, bonds, fine art, and even foreign currencies. Through speculation, you're essentially making a bet that an asset is going to appreciate in value in a short period of time. Speculation isn't based on intrinsic value of the asset, but on its price movement in the market.

With speculation, the risk of loss is more than offset by the possibility of a substantial gain or other recompense. Some market pros view speculators as gamblers.

Speculation and gambling are two different actions used to increase wealth under conditions of risk or uncertainty. Gambling refers to wagering money in an event that has an uncertain outcome in hopes of winning more money, whereas speculation involves taking a calculated risk with an uncertain outcome. Speculation involves some sort of positive expected return on investment, even though the end result may very well be a loss. The expected return for gambling is negative for the player, even though some people may get lucky and win.

Gambling in the markets is often evident in people who do it mostly for the emotional high they receive from the excitement and action of the markets. Relying on emotion, or a must-win attitude, to create profits rather than trading in a methodical and tested system, indicates the person is gambling in the markets through speculation and is unlikely to succeed over the course of many trades.

The point I am trying to make is that you can be involved in any type of investment, but do it responsibly. Gain the right knowledge if you're going to speculate in the markets, and seek professional advice. It's useful to create a checklist of steps you should follow, or rules, so that you aren't lost in emotional reactions. If an action is not on the checklist, then you know not to do it.

Day trading and foreign exchange

Day trading is another type of investing behavior. It can be extremely profitable, and high-risk profile traders can generate huge percentage returns even overnight.

Day trading describes making many transactions over the course of one day, some that are profitable and others that aren't, but with the intention that added together, the transactions will will have made money for the day trader.

Day trading is a mentally and psychologically challenging activity and is by no means meant for everyone. As you know from my story, I became an amateur day trader, and suffered greatly for it, not just financially, but also health-wise.

Foreign exchange is profiting off the conversion of one country's currency into another. Every day, trillions of dollars exchange currency through governments, travelers, businesses, banks, and speculators. Every transaction presents an opportunity for investors to make money in foreign exchange.

The primary challenges of investing

As I'm sure you can tell from those short descriptions, these forms of investing have some downsides. Let's build upon our knowledge by understanding the four primary challenges of traditional investments, which are:

- Uncertainty
- Low returns
- Stress
- A lack of purpose and engagement

Challenge #1: Investing is uncertain

Every investor balances their risk tolerance with their desire to make money. In traditional investing, the higher the risk, the greater the potential return. Of course, on the flip side, the higher the risk the greater the potential loss!

Speculation directs trillions of dollars to stock markets, foreign exchange, digital currencies, and the trading industry. Every single dollar is someone's hard-earned work, and it's being gambled on the chance that they'll make it big. The thing about speculation is someone needs to lose potential value for another person to win it. Not everyone can come out on top.

Investors in speculative markets are playing by someone else's rules. You can lose it all by one "throw of the dice."

Remember how we talked about the importance of controlling the particles in an investment? Let's consider the number of particles in a traditional stock market investment: they might include the CEO's leadership, all the C-level decisions, manager decisions, client movements, vendor performance, natural disasters, press releases…the particles are innumerable. And in order for an investment to do well, they have to be aligned in a positive direction for a good moment to happen. Even the CEO can't control all of the particles, much less investors!

When you invest your money in the stock market, you're essentially stepping into the middle of a tornado of variables. It's possible that your cash portfolio will work its way through the tornado unharmed, or will even increase in size by collecting additional cash blowing about in the storm. However, it's also possible that the tornado will sweep your cash away and deposit it somewhere far outside your reach, and you never see it again.

It's important for you to at least know what you're getting yourself into. If you're going to step into a tornado, do so with the full knowledge of what that means. There are people who know how to stay safe in the middle of a tornado, just as there are people who know how to safely dive with sharks.

Are these divers still putting their lives at risk? Yes. Have they prepared as much as possible and are making an informed, calculated decision? Yes. Do they know what can happen if just one shark feels threatened or behaves unpredictably? Yes.

In any extreme sport—from surfing eighty-foot waves, to cliff jumping, to kayaking over waterfalls—the athletes have fallen in love with the game. They learned the rules, the objective, and how to increase their chances of success, and they've dedicated time to training. There's still a risk, and the game is still filled with uncertainty, but they choose it anyway.

You need to ask yourself: how much uncertainty are you willing to engage in when it comes to your wealth? Do you want to be able to control as many particles as possible, or are you willing to step into the tornado?

At the end of the day, the stock market cannot be predicted. Sure, investors make theories, and they look at trends, but no one can know the exact moment when the market will crash, or when a stock will go up. Only in hindsight do we see patterns. For many investors, this uncertainty is something they constantly struggle with. Are they willing to risk their retirement or their children's future if they're just as likely to lose their money as double it?

When we talk about Housing PhilanthroInvesting, you will see that the model has been built to control as many particles as possible!

Challenge #2: Returns are low

A lot of people I work with have stories about their parents or grandparents hiding cash in all sorts of nooks and crannies around their homes. They didn't trust the banks. They didn't trust the stock market. So, they put rolled-up cash in their socks, or under mattresses. They didn't care if their money lost value over time. They wanted to know it was safe.

For a lot of investors, they feel like there are only two ends of a spectrum: either you hide cash throughout your house and suffer depreciating value, or you take on high risk with the hopes of good returns. The greatest middle ground they can find is investing in a government bond, where the returns are dismally low, but the "safety" of the money is more certain.

The truth is, investors want to make money. If they didn't, they wouldn't be investing their money! All investors calculate the return on their investment and work to build a portfolio that demonstrates healthy growth. If their returns are low, or if they even end up losing money, that investor might have been better off cutting a hole in the mattress and hiding their cash!

Challenge #3: The stress of investing

There are too many horrific stories to count about the stress of investing. The most severe cases make the news, and stand out as cautionary tales.

In 2020, a 20-year-old died by suicide because he borrowed and lost $730,000 in the stock market. Alexander E. Kearns was a student at the University of Nebraska. When the global COVID-19 pandemic struck, Kearns took up investing with a millennial-focused brokerage firm called Robinhood. Kearns was able to take out almost a million dollars of leverage and started speculating in the market as it swung wildly in the waves of the pandemic.

It wasn't until his parents found him, and a final note on his computer, that anyone realized what had happened. When Kearns saw that large amount of money in red, it was too much to take. In his final note, Kearns criticized Robinhood for allowing a young person with no experience to speculate in ways that could negatively impact their future livelihood.

It's not only young people who are at risk of life-changing stress from investing. I watched a friend of mine lose a large amount of money in the market. From there on it was one bad chain-reaction of events after another. He lost his marriage. His physical health, which had been immaculate due to his daily commitment to the gym, took a turn for the worst because of depression and overeating. Seeking to numb the pain, he quickly became morbidly obese.

Stress can compound, and before we know it, our bad decisions in the marketplace spill over into our lives. Even the most rational of people start making irrational choices, all in the name of earning back the money that they lost. When our scale of "normal" skews so far into debt, it's hard to see things clearly. And for some, poor sleep and poor health outcomes are the least of their worries in the face of emotional and spiritual crises.

Is this really how we want our relationship with our money to be? This was exactly how I felt when I lost my money in the foreign exchange and stock markets almost overnight, and it was the impetus for developing PhilanthroInvesting. The purpose of life is so much greater and richer than the accumulation of cash. I don't think anyone should ever lose their life, or their health, or their relationships, because of the stress of compulsive cash accumulation through "investing" or gambling.

Challenge #4: Traditional investing lacks purpose and true engagement

The truth is, if you aren't engaged with your investments, you won't have control. The game becomes money for the sake of money. As our survey revealed, many investors want more options than that.

Consider this scenario: you're working with a financial advisor. You ask him, "Mr. John, can you tell me what funds I'm investing in, please?"

He provides the specific names and performance metrics of your investments, and how much money you have in each asset.

Now you say, "Why that asset?" He gives you information about a company and their product, their mission, and their plans for the future. Then you ask, "Who is the CEO?" You get the person's name, and you search for them on Google. You see they have three kids, a partner, and love hiking outdoors and helping orphaned kids on the weekends. This person is engaged with their society and living from a place of purpose.

That helps *you* feel engaged and living from a place of purpose! You realize that not only are you investing in your own future, but you're investing in the future of these orphaned kids who are being helped. You feel emotionally connected to this person, and by proxy, the company. You are helping create something you care about in the world.

Do you see the difference between this approach to investing with emotional engagement and purpose versus passively looking at numbers? What I'm trying to communicate here is, don't just look at the numbers. Look at the real life facts creating and supporting the numbers.

Do you see how the investing options shared above lack these layers?

Speculation won't fix these challenges, because it never has

If we look at the four challenges of investing—uncertainty, low returns, the stress of investing, and the lack of purpose and engagement—I think we can safely say that speculation isn't the solution to these challenges. In fact, if we turn to history, we find that the destabilization of speculation goes way back. The best way to understand the present situation is to reflect on past patterns.

History's first speculative bubble

The goal of speculation is to profit off of price changes. If you buy while a commodity, good, or stock is low, you want to sell when it's high. However, the market does not always satisfy this desire, and speculators can contribute to financial bubbles that have far-reaching implications.

Take, for example, the first well-documented speculative bubble: tulip mania (also known as tulip madness, tulip bubble, tulip fever, or tulip hysteria). This was a period in the Golden Age of the Netherlands, during which tulip bulbs became the object of speculation.

Tulips had been a luxury item since their introduction to the Netherlands in the second half of the 16th century. They were exclusive commodities, cultivated in the gardens of the upper class, scholars, and aristocrats. The price of a single flower grew so high, it cost more than some houses and higher than some local workers' annual income. Contracts were created to trade in the ownership of tulips, making the sales easier because investors didn't always have to transport the flowers.

As the demands for tulips grew, farmers planted more to provide enough supply. The prices grew so high that finally, the market couldn't support it anymore. With a lack of buyers who could pay the extraordinary price of tulips and an over-supply of flowers, the market collapsed abruptly at the beginning of February 1637. Greediness and hype drove the prices of the flowers so high that it led to panic and fear, typical emotional swings that are involved in financial bubbles and crashes.

A pattern that repeats

This trend has been seen time and again. The 1920s experienced a severe crash when stocks appreciated to an unsustainable level (including stocks in radio companies like Radio Corporation of America, RCA) before crashing, which signaled the beginning of the Great Depression.

The pattern again repeated in the 1960s, which saw a group of companies emerge that became known as the "Nifty Fifty." These were regarded as one-decision stocks whose businesses were so powerful that all one needed to do was to buy and hold them forever. They included such household names as Xerox, Polaroid, Eastman Kodak, and Walmart. Not only did these companies have attractive growth rates, but they also possessed strong competitive positions.

Once again, the prices rose to unreasonable amounts. The 1970s saw deflation in the valuations of the 1960s. Investors again learned that purchase price matters, and that simply buying well-known companies is not necessarily a path to superior investment results.

To put it into perspective, there have been almost sixty crashes in four of the world's major indexes since 1950. One of the most notable in recent memory was the 2008 housing crash.

The 2008 housing crash

Considering our history, there were warning signs before the 2008 housing crash, such as the rapid rise of speculation by the public, which started buying and flipping second and third houses. Credit standards were relaxed so that practically anyone could get a mortgage. The originators of these mortgages seemingly went out of their way to sell mortgages to customers who had little realistic hope of ever repaying them based on their income. Why should the banks have cared? They weren't going to keep the mortgage and be on the hook for any losses; they were going to sell the debt to others.

The signs were only recognized by a few, but it didn't make a difference to the public at large.

The big underlying assumption—that house prices could not decline at the national level—was the mantra on which the whole house of cards was built. But what is true at one price was no longer true at another. House prices had never severely declined in the past; that was true. However, house prices had never been so high relative to various measures of affordability, such as income or rent.

The subsequent collapse in house prices almost destroyed the financial system. A number of financial companies failed or were sold off at deeply distressed prices as a way to limit the damage. The recession that ensued was accompanied by stock prices changing from exuberant to distressed. Investors were yet again reminded that the purchase price of an investment always matters, no matter how attractive the underlying business or asset.

Are we in a new bubble?

More than a decade since the Great Recession of 2008 began, the environment has again changed from despondent to very optimistic. Are we in a bubble? Are stock prices highly irrational? Those questions are very hard to answer in real-time. Yet there are some signs that indicate investors might be once again purchasing stocks beyond what is reasonable or sustainable. Only time will tell.

What we *do* know is that markets crash. It is a reliable cycle in the whole process—we just don't know *when*.

As we consider the four challenges of investing, it is clear that speculation does not offer satisfactory solutions. It remains uncertain, with unpredictable returns, can be stress-inducing, and at times in our history, these crashes have created terrible implications for people around the world. The 2008 housing crash wasn't just an interesting story featured in the news. It was a lived experience for many people whose financial livelihoods were suddenly destitute. Others found themselves homeless or without a job and saddled with debts that needed paying. If the banks providing the mortgages had truly had people's best interests at heart—and if they'd led from a place of purpose and emotional engagement—I'd wager that things would have worked out differently.

Whether or not we're in a new bubble, the truth is that the market will continue to fluctuate up and down, sometimes in big ways. And for investors who look at this pattern and feel uneasy with their options, there's another path.

A new solution to speculation

I know that speculation won't go away. If that's the course someone wants to take with their money, I want them to walk that path with knowledge and confidence.

My goal with this book isn't to convince you one way or the other, but to offer a new solution to those who look at this history of speculation and believe it isn't worthy of their money or time. In my experience, speculation impacts the quality of people's lives—it's volatile and makes promises it can't keep, it lacks the right engagement, and, perhaps most importantly, it draws our focus to the wrong things.

For the PhilanthroInvestor, it's not just about making money —it's about fulfillment and purpose. PhilanthroInvestors recognize that no human really needs three Lamborghinis and two Ferraris. They know that the seductive illusion of material success is just that: an illusion.

Instead, PhilanthroInvestors wonder how they can improve the world, for themselves and the people around them. They want to leave the planet better than they found it, rather than taking from it in excess.

PhilanthroInvestors approach their financial legacy from a place of abundance, not scarcity, and in doing so they can address all four challenges investors face.

If you want to invest in speculative investments, that's totally your choice! I would recommend you invest no more than 1% of your net worth, and then reinvest your profit cash flow in PhilanthroInvesting!

And this leads us to the next chapter, where we will review how to identify an ideal investment, the path to wealth, and after that, how we can go beyond ideal investments into true financial freedom.

Take a Moment to PhilanthroInvest

Is some of your wealth currently invested in stocks, bonds, traditional real estate, or other types of traditional investments? What has your experience been? Are you satisfied with them?

_____

_____

_____

_____

_____

The four primary challenges of investing are uncertainty, low returns, stress, and a lack of purpose and engagement. Do you experience any of these challenges?

_____

_____

_____

_____

As you think about the patterns of speculative bubbles and subsequent crashes, does that create greater enthusiasm for investing in the market, or less? Why?

_____

_____

_____

_____

How did your country's last economic crisis affect you? Do you know anyone who was significantly impacted? Could they have avoided it?

_____

_____

_____

_____

Chapter 3
The Path to True Financial Freedom

Not all investments are made equal. I realize we just spent a chapter reviewing the challenges in investing, but that doesn't mean you shouldn't invest! My goal is to equip you with knowledge so that you can make your own decisions. And that knowledge includes how to identify an ideal investment.

Ideal investments are based on life essentials

Although it seems like common sense, I'm amazed by how many investors don't think about the desirability of an investment in relation to what humanity needs. (You won't be surprised to learn this is one of the principles for Philanthro-Investing!).

Humans will always need water. They will always need homes, and clean air, and food, and clothing, and energy, and health, and creativity.

When you invest in the fundamental needs of humanity, you empower society. How do you know if something is a fundamental need? If it creates better futures for humankind, then you are contributing to something important.

Not only does this empower society, but it's a smart investment. We will always need that essential item, which inherently makes the investment low risk, potentially high in returns, emotionally engaging, and valuable.

When assessing whether an investment is ideal, start by asking yourself whether this is a massively-needed item and if it will create better futures. Assets are "valuable things." If you invest in things that will increase in value and importance as humanity continues to improve, then you're making a sound decision. And if wealth is a plentiful supply of a particularly desirable thing ("desirable" means things that are attractive, useful, or necessary), then you want to invest your assets there.

The ten characteristics of an ideal investment

The ten characteristics of an ideal investment include metrics that all investors want (like a high return on investment, and low risk), as well as some less-considered characteristics (like a turnkey operation, or a useable currency). These ten characteristics can serve as a guide for assessing whether an investment is ideal or not. You want to make sure that your investment complies with all, or almost all, of the characteristics.

1. Low risk
2. Double-digit ROI
3. Capital gains
4. Tax advantages
5. Double-digit cash on cash return
6. High stability
7. Outperform your currency to support and enhance your life
8. Turnkey
9. Based on life essentials
10. Backed by a physical asset

#1: Low risk

Obviously, the goal when investing is to make money, not lose it. *You don't have to lose money when investing!* If you have an investment that's low risk, you can rest assured that your money is safe.

Often, investments are seen as either high risk and high ROI, or low risk and low ROI. It is possible to have an investment that is low risk and high ROI! Some of the characteristics below—like an investment backed by an asset—create the right formula to achieve this.

#2: Double-Digit ROI

If you have cash sitting in a bank account, it's likely losing value over time due to the rise in inflation. Bank accounts often have very low-interest rates.

You want your money to grow in value while you are wearing your investor hats. You want to access your investment below the immediate market value, generating double-digit ROI from the moment you acquire it, or at least in the first year of holding it. The double-digits refer to the percentage of the ROI, as calculated in Chapter 2. (A 10% ROI would be double-digit, whereas a 5% ROI would be single.)

#3: Capital gain

Capital gain, as we reviewed in Chapter 2, is what creates ROI. Some countries give tax benefits for realized capital gains over twelve months. You want those benefits. Wearing the holder investor hat for capital gain purposes can be very beneficial.

#4: Tax advantages

As we discussed in the seven factors of investing, I would recommend working with a skilled accountant to understand what tax advantages exist for your investments. By knowing those rules, you can then assess whether an investment is ideal or not based on its potential tax benefits. Often, investments decrease your taxable income. The more money you can keep, the wealthier your future will be.

#5: Double digits cash on cash return

An ideal investment has double digits cash on cash return. If you remember the three types of cash flow, an ideal investment has a strong *profit* cash flow, which is the amount of money beyond what you invested in the asset.

Depending on the investor hat you're wearing (which we will explore below), that cash flow might come through different means and at different intervals. You might receive monthly interest payments, which is your profit cash flow. Or, you might trade an asset for cash after it grows in value over years.

Each investor hat has an opportunity to produce profit cash flow, and an ideal investment fits your desired amount and frequency of cash flow. At the end of the deal, you want to have received at least a double-digit ROI and a double-digit cash on cash return.

#6: High stability

Investments are for the future, but life is happening now. As it turns out, for most people, life is quite unpredictable. Even more so if someone doesn't plan for their future. You don't always know when things are going to happen, or where your goals might take you next. What if you want to switch careers, or your parent falls ill and you want to move closer to them? What if your child decides to go to a private university and you've promised to pay for their schooling? How can you structure your investments to be supportive of an enjoyable present moment, and future moments?

An ideal investment is highly stable, which allows you to live a better life now *and* in the future.

This means you know your cash flow projections for the next

twelve months because they are steady. If you know what you're going to earn a year from now, it's much easier to plan your life and remain flexible in the face of the unknown.

#7: Outperform your currency

One of my goals with PhilanthroInvesting is to empower you to support communities in your home country. I live in the U.S., but I'm sharing this knowledge to improve the lives of families and communities around the world so that my fellow humans can be uplifted into greater wealth. I want to invite as many people as possible along my wide Purpose Line.

When you invest, you want your cash flow to come in a currency that is useable to fulfill your dreams and goals, and to create a better future for you and others. To accomplish this, you want your investments to outperform your local usable currency by beating inflation.

Sometimes people want to participate in other currencies. It can be useful, but please keep in mind what you can do to support your home country.

#8: Turnkey

Turnkey is a descriptive word that means "the provision of a complete product or service that is ready for immediate use." It's like a comprehensive, workable system.

With a turnkey investment (also called a turnkey business), the investment itself has already been established. It's proven to work the same way throughout time, thanks to an established system with knowledgeable people and tools to support it.

For example, a restaurant franchise is a turnkey business. The parent company provides a template for how to start this business. They have data, experts, proven strategies, and tools to help your business launch. You are more likely to be successful as a franchise owner than if you were to start a business completely from scratch, with no previous experience.

In an ideal investment, we want those same variables.

Look deeply into each investment and assess the systems behind the investment.

You will understand more about turnkey businesses in Chapter 6 when I share about Equity & Help, the first Housing PhilanthroInvesting company in the world, located in the United States.

#9: Based on life essentials

You already learned what the life essentials are in Chapter 2. Well, this point is simple. Make sure that you engage with and support an investment based on any of the life essentials. It will help you navigate the sea of investments.

#10: Backed by a physical asset

An ideal investment is backed by a real asset, which means your money isn't just floating around—it's concrete. You own a physical house, or you own physical gold, or you own valuable artwork or equipment. Even if your ownership is expressed through paper, that paper is backed by a real asset. When you have an investment backed by a physical asset, even if the value of that asset goes down for a while—as housing prices did in the 2008 crash—you can continue holding onto the asset until it recovers. And because you ensured this investment is performing double-digit cash on cash return, you won't be as worried when its value fluctuates in a crisis.

If your investment isn't backed by a physical asset, your future is at greater risk.

The path to wealth

If you don't know how to invest your money, or what things to look for in an investment, you won't be able to establish a strong foundation for your path to wealth. Beyond inheritance and earning money through a job, wealth can only be created through investing. If your investments meet those ten characteristics, you're much more likely to protect and enhance your future.

Now, what is this path to wealth I keep talking about? Well, there are five steps, each building on the previous.

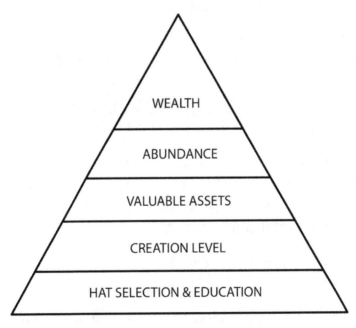

Obviously, the Path To Wealth ends in "wealth," but as you know, this book is about PhilanthroInvesting and how to make the world a better place. I call this "true financial freedom,"

which is a step beyond wealth. Once we go through these five steps, I'll tell you what true financial freedom is, and how PhilanthroInvesting is the key to reaching it.

The investor hats

Although we use the word "investor" liberally, there are different ways to invest your assets, all with the goal of increasing your wealth.

I call these different forms of investing "hats." You can easily take them off and put another on. You might switch between a number of different investor hats, just as you wear different identities throughout your day. In one day, you might be a parent, a spouse, a boss, a friend, a cook, and a customer. The longer you live, the more identities you gather.

All of the hats require education, and the more workable education you obtain, the easier you will climb the stairs in your path to wealth

The six investor hats are: lender, leaser, trader, holder, enhancer, and entrepreneur.

These hats make up the base of the path to wealth, which starts with the act of investing. The more knowledge you have in a hat, the more skilled you will be as an investor, because you know how best to control that investment.

This is how we start our journey.

Hat #1: Lender

A lender is an organization or person that lends money. The person to whom they lend money pays them back the original principal amount, and the lender earns profit cash flow through interest payments.

The most basic example of a lender is a bank. The bank loans people money to buy a house, or build a house, or buy a car, and that amount is paid back over time with interest.

There's a real advantage to wearing the lender hat. As you will see in chapters to come, the lender often ends up on top, assuming smaller risk with the possibility for great returns. The lender also has the security of a physical asset behind their investment (like a house, or a car).

Hat #2: Leaser

The leaser is a person who possesses an asset and leases that asset to someone else for a specific amount of time and money. You can lease many things in the investing world, like cars, equipment, and real estate. (Leasing can also be thought of as "renting.")

If a person wants to lease a car rather than buying one, they save money in the short term and can test the car without making a large purchase. Equipment stores lease items like carpet cleaners so that homeowners don't need to purchase something they use infrequently.

A leaser generates profit when they start earning cash above what they paid to acquire the asset. For example, if the leaser purchased a carpet cleaner for $3,000, and they rent it for $100/day, they will need to rent the carpet cleaner for thirty days to recover their original cash. All of the cash after that is profit cash flow, and can be reinvested in another asset to continue growing wealth.

Hat #3: Trader

The trader hat is as old as our economy. People traded assets to acquire other assets, like an item of clothing for loaves of bread. Originally, for the average person, trading was a means of obtaining life essentials, not a means of growing wealth.

When we talk about the trading hat in investing, it's a slightly different story. A trader exchanges their asset for something else, hoping the new asset will be of greater value than what they gave away.

The trouble with trading is that both parties think they got the better deal (otherwise they wouldn't have traded!), but usually only one will be right. If trading reminds you of speculation, you would be right—trading is a form of speculation. At least on a short-term basis, it is a zero-sum game, has substantial risk, but could have high rewards.

To be effective, traders need to have keen knowledge in order to evaluate each trade. Are they getting the better deal? Do they have experience with this kind of trade? Do they know the market or industry well?

If I trade these two cars for that one car, will I be able to find someone who will pay a higher price for it? Or will I need to fix it up to increase its value (which is another hat, the enhancer)?

When people trade on the stock market, it's often called "day trading," because this individual makes a lot of trades within the course of a single day. If one of their trades is unfavorable, they need to execute other trades to recover the loss. Trading is often characterized by a lot of transactions for a small amount of gains that add up over time. A day trader's goal is for the asset to appreciate in a short time faster than the value of the currency in which they are trading. That is how a trader makes a profit in the stock market.

If we think about the concept of trading, we realize that there is actually no such thing as "buying" or "selling" an asset. There is only ever trading assets. If you exchange your piece of real estate for another, you're trading. If you exchange your real estate for cash, you're also trading. Your new asset is cash. If you were to put that cash towards a stock, you would again be trading.

"Selling" gives the impression that something is going away. Using the word "trading" represents the understanding that our assets only ever morph into something else. Of course, assets can *lose* value through trades. In that case, we end up trading our asset for something of lesser value.

Hat #4: Holder

A holder is someone who invests in an asset and holds the asset for a long period of time, predicting that the asset will improve in value. Some examples of common assets that are held are: precious metals, art collections, classic cars, certain stocks. (If you bought Apple stock in 1999, and you've kept it until this day, that's holding).

Like the trader, the holder needs to have a masterful understanding of this asset, or this industry, to evaluate what assets are worth holding. The holder wants their asset to appreciate over time more than the inflation rate of that currency.

When the holder finally trades the asset for another asset, like cash, they will make a profit if the amount exceeds both inflation and what was originally paid to acquire it.

Hat #5: Enhancer

The enhancer uses their time, effort, and often cash to improve an existing asset so they can trade it for assets of higher value.

Enhancers always work on physical assets. If you buy a house, put cash towards improving the house, and then trade the house for more cash than the original cost and the cost of improvements, that is a form of enhancing. In the real estate industry, this is called a "fix and flip." The enhancer often enhances and trades assets as quickly as they can to grow their wealth.

Hat #6: Entrepreneur

The sixth and final hat is the entrepreneur hat. When someone wears an entrepreneur hat, they create a valuable asset, which is a company.

In Spanish, the word for entrepreneur is emprendedor, which comes from the root *emprender*, "to start something with great importance." Entrepreneurs create something that they believe is important and moves them in the direction they want—for themselves, and for society at large.

Obviously, this hat isn't for everyone; not everyone wants to be responsible for starting a company. There are many things to consider when wearing the entrepreneur hat, like hiring and being responsible for other people's lives, the job of running a company, and building a team. This book is not about entrepreneurship. If you're interested in this hat, I would recommend educating yourself so you have the knowledge to develop this asset appropriately. Of all the hats, the entrepreneur hat has the most moving particles and requires the most amount of skill.

The entrepreneur makes a profit when their company distributes dividends. The entrepreneur's most important tool is an accurate P&L (profit and loss) statement, which is a document that details a company's ability to generate profit (or not). They use the P&L statement to make business decisions that can create profit cash flow.

One final piece of advice about the entrepreneur hat: in order to make a true profit, the entrepreneur needs to operate on cash basis accounting versus accrual accounting. Cash basis will recognize revenue when cash actually comes to you, rather than when an agreement is made. Going back to our ideal investment, you want to base your investments on real, stable assets—like cash—rather than promised assets that are not yet in your hand.

Creation

Let's return to the Path To Wealth model. Once a person engages in an investment by donning a hat, they have the ability to move on to the creation level.

The creation level is associated with how much energy or effort you put into that hat. If you're a leaser and you have one apartment unit, what is your level of creation? Compare that to my friend who owns 10,000 apartment units. What's his level of creation?

To achieve greater wealth, increase your creation level in whichever hat you're wearing by acquiring more valuable assets and putting them to work.

This isn't about judgment or competition. The purpose of the path to wealth is to create the life *you* want. If you want to generate a lot of wealth, you need a strong creation engine. Elon Musk is able to accomplish so many things in his life because of his strong creation engine. If that isn't your goal, determine the effort that's right for you

Valuable assets = Money

Money, by one definition, is the amount of valuable assets you have.

A valuable asset is something that supports life essentials and produces profit cash flow.

The creation level only leads to wealth if it's generating valuable assets. If your collection of classic cars is depreciating in value because you aren't taking care of them, they won't lead to the path to wealth. If you're involved in other speculative investments that don't contribute to the life essentials, it also won't lead to the path to wealth. Instead, you're losing your valuable asset of money, not gaining it.

We need money (defined as "something generally accepted as a medium of exchange, a measure of value, or a means of payment") to generate wealth. With the power of compound interest, our money can make more money. But if we aren't making money from our assets, no matter how strong our creation engine, we will not reach wealth! An ideal investment has profit cash flow.

Abundance

As we generate the valuable asset of money, we eventually reach abundance. Abundance is merely "a very large quantity of something." It's an overflow or surplus.

The definition of wealth includes the concept of abundance. "Wealth is a plentiful supply of a particular desirable thing." We need a plentiful supply—or an abundant supply—to reach wealth. If you don't create abundance, you don't arrive at wealth.

Abundance is the byproduct of a strong creation engine that

produces a surplus of money. If you have yet to reach abundance, revisit the previous steps on our path to wealth.

Wealth

If an investor has a strong creation engine while wearing one or many of his investor hats, which produces valuable assets, while leading to an abundant supply, they will achieve wealth. But the journey doesn't end there. The investor can use that wealth to generate even more wealth, continuously growing their assets and creating the life they want.

The path to wealth takes time, engagement, knowledge, and the tools in Chapter 1. The further along the path of wealth someone journeys, the faster their wealth starts to grow.

This model, though it has a desirable destination, is actually incomplete. At least, for the PhilanthroInvestor it is. To arrive at wealth, you don't need a purpose, or to be fulfilled. You can make money for the sake of making money. But as I said before, this book is for people who want to do more with their life, and their legacy. This book is for people who know it isn't enough to have an abundance of money to spend on just themselves and their family.

How can we go beyond wealth and to the holy grail of investing: true financial freedom?

The path to true financial freedom (TFF)

The path to true financial freedom looks similar to the path to wealth, with a few distinctions: First, the only way to get to true financial freedom is through PhilanthroInvesting. This becomes your investor hat and creates a whole new foundation for investing, which we'll explore more in the next chapter. Someone can achieve wealth by investing in weapons or alcohol or speculation, but they will never reach true financial freedom. PhilanthroInvesting is about investing with a purpose, and that purpose is to generate life, not suppress it.

The second distinction: When operating from the Philanthro-Investing hat, every level on the path benefits not only you and your family, but the rest of humanity. The more you create, the more others will be helped. The more money you have, the more you can invest in a better world. And the more abundance, the greater your impact, and the wider your Purpose Line.

Finally, the destination is different. True financial freedom is beyond wealth. This is how we unlock the "well-being" part of wealth. If our abundance is just for us, I would argue that it's not true well-being because we lack connection to others, and we lack a greater purpose.

True financial freedom brings so much more to your journey than just wealth. It generates life by supporting only the life essentials.

When I think of "freedom," I see the opposite of being passive or out of control. Freedom is being active, engaged, and in control. The more knowledge you gain, the more alert you are, and the more responsibility you take for how you're living.

Life is in you. *You* are life. Not money. Money is a tool for adding to life. By freeing our finances, we also free ourselves. We can say "yes" more fully to life, and in doing so, we create beneficial ripples that stretch far and wide into the world.

True financial freedom has nine ingredients, which are:

- Knowledge
- Engagement
- Purpose
- Cash flow
- Capital growth
- Enjoyment
- Fulfillment
- Legacy
- Debt free

Knowledge

This is the first ingredient of true financial freedom is one we've discussed a few times already.

There are different phases of knowledge, and they all build on each other. Children learn to walk before they run. We learn the sounds of letters, then words, then sentences and phrases.

Knowledge compounds. We must approach investing knowledge in the same way.

In investing, the difference between not knowing something and truly knowing can be great. This is how investors end up losing hundreds of thousands of dollars. Because that gap between what they know and don't know is big enough for their wealth to leak through.

Knowledge is like a capacity-builder. The more you know, the greater your capacity to invest, and the greater your competency.

Control

Control is the act of moving particles on the planet. It is different than supervision, which is observing particles moving in the physical universe. The more engagement you have with your PhilanthroInvestment, the more decisions you will be able to make, and the more control you will have.

Engagement and purpose

Engagement follows passion and curiosity. If you're passionate about something, or you're curious, you will be naturally engaged.

The more we engage with our lives and our activities, the greater clarity we have about our purpose. And the more clarity we have about our purpose, the faster we can travel our Purpose Line towards our ultimate goal.

It's worth noting that engagement is not a passive thing. It's an active choice. We can choose to be engaged. Every time we meet someone new—whether it's an interview with a possible employer or a connection through a friend—we have two choices: we can either go into that interaction already feeling an affinity for this person, or we can choose to be suspicious and shut ourselves down.

Our mindsets are strong. If we enter that interaction with preemptive negative feelings, it's likely we will create that reality throughout the interaction. Maybe we notice how this person bounces their leg when they talk, and we use that as evidence for our further dislike.

However, if we enter a conversation or new relationship feeling a great affinity for someone, we are much more likely to enjoy their company and build a positive relationship going forward.

Imagine how much more engaged employees would be if they developed an affinity for their work! Instead of showing up every day feeling like they're somehow forced to be there, they would feel excited about their job and would bring a new level of engagement to what they did. They might even get promoted, and bring greater value to their co-workers and customers!

Ultimately, our engagement comes down to a choice. Are we going to feel positively towards this investment, and participate in it fully? Or are we going to sit back and blame others when we lose money? I think success in investing starts here: with the choice of our affinity.

In the end, it will be much easier to achieve your purpose if you chose to have the right mindset!

Cash flow and capital growth

Like an ideal investment, true financial freedom has profit cash flow, which is the flow of cash from an investment that exceeds the original amount.

True financial freedom also includes capital growth, which is an increase in the value of your asset over time. If you sell a home as a private lender with owner financing, you receive profit cash flow each month in the form of interest payments from the borrowers. You also receive capital growth, which is the difference between the amount you paid to purchase the home and what you sold it for to the family, which is now reflected in the principal balance of the loan.

Enjoyment and fulfillment

The enjoyment and fulfillment we experience in true financial freedom come as a result of our engagement. These ingredients go hand in hand. The greater our knowledge, and engagement, and purpose, the more we will enjoy our investments, and the more fulfillment we'll feel in our lives by watching life essentials grow.

The bigger our Purpose Line, the bigger our gratification.

Legacy

Most people want to leave behind some kind of legacy after they die. They want to pass on something valuable or be remembered a certain way. They want to feel proud of their lives and know that whatever positive impact they had will continue to reverberate after they're gone.

A PhilanthroInvestor has the opportunity to leave two kinds of legacies: a financial legacy, and a purpose legacy. They can rest assured that their families will be supported financially and that their memory will be associated with making the world a better place because of how they invested.

Debt-free

A responsible investor uses the knowledge and tools in this book to grow their wealth in such a way that they don't need to borrow money from banks to fund their investments. Their liabilities are low. Their profit cash flow is high.

Not everyone is able to start with a debt-free portfolio. If you need to go into debt, keep growing your wealth while reducing your liabilities so that you can eventually reach true financial freedom.

Take a Moment to PhilanthroInvest

Ideal investments support life essentials. What life essentials have you used this week? Do you see the benefit of investing in life essentials?

_____

_____

_____

_____

The path to wealth starts with wearing one of the six investor hats (lender, leaser, trader, holder, enhancer, and entrepreneur). Which of these hats have you worn before, or are wearing now?

_____

_____

_____

_____

The more creation energy we put into our investing journey, the greater our wealth will be. To what degree are you interested in creating valuable assets? What other things in your life take creation energy right now?

_____

_____

_____

_____

The path to true financial freedom goes beyond wealth. It's not money for the sake of money, but money for the sake of a better world. Does that destination appeal to you? Which of the ten ingredients of true financial freedom could you improve in your investment portfolio (knowledge, control, engagement, purpose, cash flow, capital growth, enjoyment, fulfillment, legacy, and debt-free)?

_____

_____

_____

_____

How many generations do you predict your current wealth will serve? How many generations would you like to serve?

_____

_____

_____

_____

Do you feel you are leaving a legacy for your next generation, or just an investment?

_____

_____

_____

_____

Chapter 4
PhilanthroInvesting

When we look at the world today, we see some dire statistics.

Only 8% of the world's population lives in environments with good air quality. Six thousand kids die every day from water-related diseases, and more people die from unsafe drinking water than war. Billions of families worldwide will never own their homes. Almost a billion people do not have access to electricity, and even more people are illiterate. The animal population has declined nearly 70% in fifty years, and 1.5 million animals are euthanized every year just in the U.S.

Almost 1 billion humans suffer from hunger, and contrary to that, 1.3 billion tons of food is wasted every single year and some people suffer from obesity. Health issues are rampant and over 95% of the world's population has health problems. And these statistics only reflect the world in 2020. They are constantly changing, and most only continue to worsen.

These problems—and many more—impact our core needs, our life essentials. We need clean air and water; we need health; we need shelter; the other beings with whom we share this planet deserve life.

We did not arrive at this world by accident. The current dynamics are reflections of an interconnected process. A modern world is created through the birth of many ideas. Some ideas die out, others get iterated upon, and some are implemented, then fed. The more energy and attention put into that idea, the more it grows.

Both good and bad ideas are proliferated by collective attention. We all carry a degree of responsibility for the current situations in the world. Whether knowingly or unknowingly, we have participated in ideas and systems that have led to the decline of our planet, and have prevented the equitable distribution of resources worldwide.

I say this not to cause despair, but to empower you. You and I and everyone else have the power to change the course of the world if we approach our global problems with a spirit of connection, engagement, and diligent responsibility.

But first, in order to be free of something, you need a new direction.

The power of attention for a better world

If our current world has been created through the influence of ideas, attention, and resources, that's exactly the path we need to take for a solution. What the world needs is a new game of investing.

The current game impacts not just investors, but entire countries and systems. The objective of the current game is to make money. This is why we have healthcare industries ruled by insurance companies. The system is not set up to treat the root cause of disease; it's created to turn a profit through the mitigation of symptoms. Similarly, although the housing market was created to help families become homeowners, its purpose has shifted: to profit banks and other lenders only, even if it means evicting families with children from homes and destabilizing neighborhoods.

In order to be free of the current establishments, we need to shift our attention—and our money—away from speculative investments and towards something more holistic. Something with a purpose.

There are only two hats that can precipitate this shift: the PhilanthroInvestor hat and the social entrepreneur hat.

PhilanthroInvestors can shift their wealth, and by doing so, help others while making a financial return. The social entrepreneur can step outside the dynamics of an existing world to create new businesses that operate for the world of tomorrow. Their businesses support life essentials, and they can even get the support of PhilanthroInvestors across the globe. Behind a PhilanthroInvesting company are social entrepreneurs who founded and run that company. They don't need to wait for progress in industries or governments in order to birth solutions.

Both hats, when worn this way, bring their attention to how the ailments of the world impact us all. We all need clean air; we all need stable structures that can protect us from natural disasters. Think about the kinds of feats humanity has accomplished—we sent a man to the moon! We are investigating moving to a different planet! We are not lacking in ingenuity; what we suffer from are outdated games fed by our attention and assets.

The PhilanthroInvestor and the social entrepreneur know that we have the power to reverse the story of *this* planet, and to protect the lives of those already here, and those yet to come.

This is why I'm on a mission to awaken the PhilanthroInvestor within. I believe everyone has the potential to read this, feel moved, and decide they want to play a different game. PhilanthroInvestors recognize we have an inherent responsibility to leave the world better than we found it, and they're going to take the steps to do so. They value this goal more than having three mansions, five luxury cars, two yachts, a private jet, fifty purses, fifty luxury suits, and fifty pairs of shoes. They care about this planet and making life here sustainable for everyone before doing tourism to another planet.

I believe that these problems won't be fixed solely by governments or corporations. It's also up to us to invest our time and money, and to engage emotionally to promote human welfare.

PhilanthroInvesting—the best of both worlds

The more people we free from the speculative investment world, the greater energy and attention they will have for PhilanthroInvesting. These same investors can PhilanthroInvest without sacrificing their financial return.

You can imagine PhilanthroInvesting at the center point of a linear scale with "philanthropy" on the far left, and "traditional investing" on the far right.

Philanthropy is all about having a social purpose and fulfillment, but it's not meant to be financially sustainable. On the other end of the spectrum, traditional investments are all about making a financial return and have nothing to do with purpose. Philanthropists on the left give grants to social purpose organizations that do not have a self-sustaining financial model, and they leave all the fulfillment of their philanthropy to that organization's staff. Investors on the right hope to make money passively, not engaging with their wealth, and experiencing money for the sake of money, which is far from true happiness.

Even when it comes to impact investments—which are companies, organizations, or funds that have an intention to benefit the environment and society—the primary purpose is still to make money. The impact is a small portion of what most of those companies or funds do.

PhilanthroInvesting sits right in the middle of this spectrum and represents the best of both worlds. It's about investing in social purpose organizations with proven financial business models, and making it an ideal investment. As a PhilanthroInvestor, you're engaged and knowledgeable so that you can be the CEO of your portfolio, making the right decisions for what you want to accomplish in relation to the Purpose Line you've chosen.

The traditional investment is going to die

I believe in a world where individuals fully value their resources; a world where people don't speculate, and only PhilanthroInvest.

I believe the traditional investment will eventually die. We won't "invest" anymore, we'll only "PhilanthroInvest." The more investors realize that we support what we help create, the more our consciousness level will rise, and the more responsibility we'll feel for the world we're creating. PhilanthroInvesting will become the only game because it satisfies two desires: the desire to walk a wider Purpose Line, and the desire to grow wealth.

My hope is that, in this transition away from speculation, we will also reduce and eliminate gambling. More than 450 billion dollars are gambled every year worldwide. That money could be redistributed where it is needed, rather than being thrown away in a low-consciousness activity. Not only is the person who gambles losing their own future, they're sacrificing the potential for others to have meaningful, healthy futures, too.

The natural laws of betterment and giving back

I believe there are natural laws that govern our universe. If we abide by these laws, our lives are improved.

For example, if you playfully toss a young child up into the air, then catch them, you will both experience immense enjoyment. That joy is evident in the child's big smile and giggles. This is gravity at work, but also the sheer delight in connection, play, and safety.

Another natural law I believe in is the "natural law of betterment." Simply put, as the circumstances of your life improve so too does the quality, which results in improvements for the lives of people around you. And vice versa—when the lives of others improve, so does yours. This is particularly true for neighboring countries. When the conditions of a neighboring country improve, yours improve as well, and vice versa.

Let's consider an example. A young woman named Amanda has an old car in need of repairs. Any time she has extra money in her paycheck, she hears this nagging internal voice telling her to put it towards the car. For Amanda, that means there is no money for fun. She finally puts some money into the car, but while at the mechanic, she learns that there are other issues, such as an oil leak and old tires. Her car has officially become a burden. Amanda is embarrassed about the state of her car. It often fails to start and has caused her to be late to work on more than one occasion. Her circumstances are less than ideal.

If we got Amanda into a nicer car—a new car with a warranty—she would be elevated to a better place. Her car would be dependable and safe, and she would be happy knowing that she could easily get from point A to point B, worry-free. Because something in Amanda's world is now in good condition, the quality of her overall life would improve as well. She would be reliable at work, see friends more, and take road trips to visit her aging parents.

When your life circumstances are improved, everyone benefits. It's just a natural law.

Another natural law is the law of giving back: by giving to others, we receive purpose and well-being.

It feels good to help someone. We feel lighter and more connected. We feel valuable. Even if there are challenges in our lives, we know we can contribute to the world in meaningful ways, no matter how small.

Many investors see this but don't get it. Instead, they buy property in the Cayman Islands and three Lamborghinis, and they still don't feel happy. Why do they need three Italian sportscars? Why do they need one in each color? None of these material toys are impacting the law of betterment, because these excessive material items aren't actually markedly improving their lives or the lives of the people around them. Sure, it's fine to have toys, one sports car, and one sports utility vehicle (SUV) if you can afford it without debt, but when do you start turning your attention outward, to the well-being of others? When do you choose to allocate funds to a better place, like supporting a family in becoming homeowners?

Warren Buffett and Bill Gates have both amassed billions of dollars. According to a new analysis by *The Chronicle of Philanthropy*, they are the most charitable American billionaires. Buffett topped the list, giving away more than $46 billion since 2000. That works out to 71% of his $65.5 billion fortune.

Gates has given away $18 billion—or 22% of his $81 billion fortune—to charity since 2000. He and Melinda Gates have donated more than twice that amount since they created their foundation in 1994, and in 2019, he donated another $4.6 billion in Microsoft stocks.

The biggest names on the planet give back and make a difference.

Mark Zuckerberg announced in a letter to his then-newborn son, Max, that he was going to give away 99% of his Facebook shares. When this was first announced in 2015, Facebook was worth $45 billion. Five years prior, he signed the "Giving Pledge" along with other tech billionaires—including Bill Gates—to give away the majority of his wealth. Since then, Mark and his wife, Priscilla Chan, have focused on personalized learning, curing diseases, and connecting people.

The universe acts in a dynamic give-and-take. Nothing stands still, including our life situations, money, romance, and health. Our bodies, minds, and thoughts are all in constant exchange with the forces of the universe. We can accelerate or maintain this exchange by giving exactly what it is we wish to receive, and trust me, the universe always gives us back more than we give. At least, that's my personal observation.

The term "affluence" means to flow in abundance. Money is a form of energy. Like the ocean's currents, financial currencies fluctuate. To stop the flow of money out of our lives means to stop the flow coming in. Giving engenders receiving. Money, like the energy that supports life, is meant to move, and if we align that movement with the natural laws of betterment and giving back, then we hack the secret to a fulfilled life.

Frank Sinatra believed the same thing. He once said, "You gotta spend it. Move it around." It is said that when Sinatra became rich, he spent money as if there was no end to it. He showed friends lavish generosity, and also routinely tipped in $100 bills.

We can say that humans are pack animals. Society is held together by reciprocity. If we do something for others, they feel a strong urge to do something in return. This is another natural law, which I call the natural law of exchange. This is also why charities send return address labels, greeting cards, or a calendar when they ask for a donation. We're more likely to give something when we receive.

I too operate my life by these natural laws.

In 2016 and 2017 combined, I earned $556K and gave more than $400K away to charity. In the next year, my net worth grew by 500%.

The fulfillment that comes with this level of giving is much higher than if that money sat in your bank account. Sure, I could have bought two Ferraris, but instead, I opted for a pre-owned Porsche with less than 30,000 miles. I purchased a car that I would actually drive and enjoy, and I had money left over to make healthy contributions to charity and to PhilanthroInvest.

The natural laws of giving back and betterment are certain. When you improve your life, then you improve the lives of others, which improves your life again. It's a circle.

I want to give investors this opportunity for fulfillment when it comes to their investments and willingness to help others. I want to share this feeling I have now from working towards something bigger. It's not just for myself, my family, or my cars; it's to help other people and to direct the planet in a more positive direction.

The importance of help—making a difference for humanity

Help means to give or receive assistance. This encompasses the simple example of lending someone a pen, to the long-term and complex example of raising a child until she is an established member of society.

Life is much better when you are helping others. In fact, when we are helping others, we ourselves experience more life. Not helping just for personal gain, or helping so that someone owes us and must reciprocate. I am talking about helping others with the sole purpose of doing a good deed. When you lift someone up, you in turn are lifted.

Early on in my development of PhilanthroInvesting—after that first family came to me asking if there was a way for them to purchase a lot they couldn't afford—another man sought help. He said that he could not afford to send his son to university to get an education. He had always dreamed of giving his son this opportunity. The reality was crushing, but he had an idea.

The man asked if he could buy a lot in my private

neighborhood, sell it to a family, and use the profit to send his son to university. The trouble was, he didn't have enough cash upfront to pay me in full. He asked if we could come to an agreement whereby, he could own the lot, pay small installments in the interim, wait a year or two for it to appreciate, and sell it. Then, he would pay me back in full with the sale. The excess would be used for his son's education.

I said yes!

This man found a family that wanted to build a house, and was able to sell the lot for a higher price than our original deal. Better yet, the family who purchased the lot was also in need of some help, so this man offered to PhilanthroInvest with them, giving them flexible terms so they could make their dream come true. Finally, the money left over after the transactions contributed to his son's attendance at university. Can you believe how much help happened as a result of this single interaction?

This man and I ended up doing a number of deals like this. Years later, I received a picture of his son driving a nice car because he was able to secure a good job thanks to his education. The gifts of PhilanthroInvesting, and the importance of help, ripple out far beyond an original transaction, improving lives. Helping others generates life. And it all starts because we recognize how important it is to extend a hand.

Take a moment and reflect on a time when you were in need and someone helped you. Was it by offering you a ride? Listening to you in a moment of need? Providing a financial loan for something important? Helping you move? How did you feel in that moment?

Now reflect on a time when you helped someone. It could be as simple as helping a child tie her shoe, or providing professional services pro bono. What did it feel like knowing that you had something to offer, and that you contributed the time and energy to improve someone's day? It felt amazing, didn't it?

I have observed that when someone has been truly helped in the past, it increases their inclination and willingness to help others. By "paying it forward," we're creating more giving members of society who will take a moment to help another person.

Helping others helps you

Helping others creates personal well-being. A person who only acts in their own best interest is consumed by self-centered thoughts. Their problems seem bigger, and their anxieties more consuming, because their only point of reference is their own life. They are stuck with a limited perspective.

When we help others, we're reminded that we're not alone on this journey. There are other people who have their own pains and their own victories. By improving the lives of others—in ways big or small—we not only feel better about ourselves, but we realize that we can create a better overall story for humanity. Our pains lessen in the face of others' pains, and our gratitude expands. Instead of focusing on all we don't have, or all that's wrong in our lives, we feel grateful for what we do have and the ability to help others.

Even people who are living in the direst of circumstances can offer a helping hand. This kind of compassion is often seen in disasters. Someone escapes terrible flooding in their home due to a hurricane, and they turn around to help their neighbors. Or someone's house catches fire and others rush to alter the firefighters and assist the family in escaping. Or a person loses a child to a drunk driver, and they dedicate the rest of their life to reducing drunk driving.

Some of the people who've faced the worst tragedies are the most generous helpers because they know what it means for someone to offer support when times are tough. For them, there is no greater feeling than extending a helping hand.

But a tragedy doesn't need to happen for you to awaken your desire to help yourself and others. You can awaken your PhilanthroInvestor within and grow your capital while helping others.

Trust your intuition

We've talked a lot about the importance of knowledge when it comes to investing. We can't have control over this process if we don't possess the right knowledge. But there's something that goes hand-in-hand with knowledge: intuition.

The truth is the knowledge we gain about investing comes primarily from other people. They have labored to gain this knowledge, and are now passing it on to us. However, we should not adopt this knowledge blindly. We also need to engage our own perception and intuition.

No one will be able to decide your purpose for you, or how wide your Purpose Line is. You cannot gain that knowledge from outside, because it exists inside. This ties in with Philanthro-Investing, the laws of betterment, and the importance of help. As you reflect on times when you've helped someone, you intuitively feel the rightness of it.

Bring that same intuition to your investments. For me, PhilanthroInvesting was born out of intuition. A family asked me for their help so they could own a home in my neighborhood. I said yes, and together we creatively figured out how to make a deal work so that both parties could get what they wanted.

Don't PhilanthroInvest because I'm telling you to. Philanthro-Invest because it feels right!

If you now have the knowledge about how to reach true financial freedom, and you also feel that PhilanthroInvesting is the intuitive path to achieve it, then you're in the right place.

And now, we will turn our attention to the area of PhilanthroInvesting that this book seeks to address: the global housing crisis.

Take a Moment to PhilanthroInvest

The law of betterment is the improvement of your life and the lives around you when your circumstances are improved. Can you think of a time when you experienced the law of betterment? How might that impact have spread?

_____

_____

_____

_____

_____

Remember the last time that you helped someone? How long ago was it? What exactly did you do? What was their response, and how did you feel afterward?

_____

_____

_____

_____

_____

When was the last time you received help from someone? Do you remember how you felt before they helped you? What did they do for you, and how did it impact your life? How did you feel after receiving their help?

_____

_____

_____

_____

_____

When was the last time you acted out of intuition? What was the result?

_____

_____

_____

_____

_____

Chapter 5
The Real Estate Crisis

Former U.S. Hall of Fame professional baseball player and U.S. Senator Jim Bunning once said, "A loving family provides the foundation children need to succeed."

Since the dawn of time, the family unit has been a key to our society as humans. When you look at early civilizations and tribes, at the center was the family collective. We were not meant to make this journey alone; we were meant to do it together, with peaceful coexistence.

As they say, home is where the heart is. Ideally, a home is a safe place of shelter, learning, security, and love. When families have unstable housing, it can lead to dire and hopeless situations. It can cause a decrease in family health and cohesion, and possibly increase criminality, suicide, abuse, and violence. Ramifications are felt throughout a neighborhood, a community, a city, a state, and even a country.

In fact, the current housing crisis is far-reaching.

The global housing crisis

Local housing crises are often self-evident. Whether renting or buying, there's a general census when prices become prohibitively high in an area. The working class is pushed out of the city center. Traffic swells as more people commute beyond the bounds of public transport to locations where rent is cheaper. Gentrification alters neighborhood ecosystems. (Gentrification is the process by which middle class or wealthy people move to poor areas, increasing property values and displacing the poorer residents.)

When we review the larger landscape of housing trends, we realize that these patterns are not only local; we are facing a global housing crisis.

Some of the wealthiest countries in the world—despite experiencing rising prosperity—are driving a wedge between the rich and the poor. Expensive cities don't have enough homes to keep up with the swell in population. As corporations and tech companies move into cities, their employees might be able to afford the cost of living, but essential workers cannot. They're either continuously pushed to the periphery of the city, or they're pushed entirely out.

In 2017, the most unaffordable cities were Hong Kong, Sydney, Vancouver, and Melbourne. London, Toronto, Brisbane, Tokyo, Singapore, Shanghai, Beijing, Moscow, and Paris were right behind. It's no surprise that some of the wealthiest countries are also low in homeownership rankings:

- Australia ranks 41st in the world, with only 65.5% homeownership
- The US ranks 42nd, with only 65.3% homeownership
- The UK ranks 43rd, with only 65.2% homeownership
- Germany ranks 51st, with only 51.5% homeownership
- Switzerland ranks 53rd, with only 43.4% homeownership

The surprising thing is that it's not only expensive cities in advanced parts of the world that are struggling with unaffordable housing. Rapidly urbanizing parts of the developing world are, in some ways, outstripping the pace of urban cities.

In 2018, the Lincoln Institute of Land Policy reported that, from a sample of more than 200 global cities, only 10% were affordable. The UN reports that more than 1.6 billion people live in inadequate housing, which includes slums and informal settlements. These kinds of substandard dwellings—which often lack electricity, running water, and basic sanitation—are the norm in some places. In Africa, over half of the population live in substandard conditions, and in India and China, nearly a quarter of the population live in informal settlements.[1]

When it comes to unaffordable housing, the least advantaged are often the most burdened. In the United States, of the households that earn less than $15,000 a year, nearly three-quarters spend more than half of their income on housing. In the Global South, the numbers are even worse. In rapidly urbanizing cities like Bogota, Buenos Aires, Rio de Janeiro, Hanoi, and Mumbai, housing costs exceed as much as 100% to 300% of the average income. And with as many as 200,000 people moving to cities in the Global South each day, these numbers are likely to get worse.[2]

When we talk about "affordable housing," what does that actually mean? It is generally agreed upon that if a household spends more than 30% of their income on housing, they are considered "cost burdened." Their housing is not affordable. The United Nations Human Settlements Programme (UN-Habitat) defines "affordable" in their sustainable urbanization program as "housing which is adequate in quality and location and does not cost so much that it prohibits its occupants from meeting other basic living costs or threatens their enjoyment of basic human rights."

---

[1] World Economic Forum

[2] Bloomberg CityLab

Between evictions, unsafe housing options, and the burden placed on vulnerable populations, some consider unaffordable housing a human rights violation. Housing should be a right, not a privilege. And yet there are many other forces standing in the way of solutions. Many of these same forces contributed to this dynamic in the first place.

How did we get here?

The global housing crisis is a multi-faceted problem. Experts cite differing causes colliding in the perfect storm.

In rapidly urbanizing cities, the middle class is being impacted by the housing crisis alongside the poor. As tech companies and other corporations move to cities, it creates a gap between knowledge-based employment and essential workers. Housing prices are rising faster than incomes, with little to no growth happening in the middle class. Between 2006 and 2014, rent in the U.S. increased 22% on average, while average income only grew 6%.[3] Teachers, police, firefighters, service workers, nurses, and others with paying jobs cannot afford to live in the communities they serve.

Not enough houses at the appropriate price point are being built to address the demand. There's an oversupply of luxury dwellings to accommodate the knowledge-based workers, but an undersupply of affordable houses for essential workers. We're facing a chronic shortage with an undercurrent of accessibility.

Another variable standing in the way is land scarcity and cost due to zoning restrictions. Certain areas in a city might be zoned

---

[3] Bloomberg CityLab

for commercial use, but not residential; or they might be zoned for single-family homes, but not multi-family units, which are more affordable when renting. As cities continue to build, there's less land available, and little to no incentives to use that land for affordable dwellings.

Affordability also goes beyond rent. People need to be able to sustain the costs of living in an area, including expenses like food, transportation, repairs, amenities (heating and cooling are more expensive in energy inefficient buildings), access to healthcare and education, and so on. Without proper infrastructure—or in the face of prohibitive expenses—housing might still not be truly affordable due to living costs. The number of urban poor is rising, as is homelessness in the U.S. Around the world, millennials are spending more money on housing than any previous generation, and suffering from a lower quality of life.[4] For those who can afford to buy homes, they're locking in housing costs and benefiting from rapid appreciation. But for those who are renting, they're facing an impossible scenario. The people who would benefit the most from homeownership aren't the ones who can access it.

Another primary driver of the crisis is the globalization of the housing market. Homeownership used to be a local industry. Homes were bought, built, and occupied by locals. However, in recent years real estate trading has contributed to a large portion of the global economy. A UN report estimates that the total value of global real estate accounts for 60% of global assets, valued at $217 trillion. Housing prices are more entwined with the global economy than ever before, creating fluctuations that mirror

---

[4] World Economic Forum

what's happening worldwide rather than local capital flow. As the ultra-rich switch their primary source of wealth from gold to high-end apartments in expensive cities, residents are driven to the outskirts.

Housing is no longer about providing safety and shelter to community members. It's about capitalizing on the real estate market as a self-oriented investor and making as much money as possible from that asset. This is a total violation of the laws of betterment, exchange, giving back, and of course, the Philanthro-Investing philosophy and purpose.

Developers also partake in the game. They have greater incentives to build expensive residences than affordable housing. It's not only about their margins when selling. In some cases, through policy, zoning, and politics, cities incentivize builders *not* to create affordable housing. Many developers also face increasing costs of materials and labor, finding it hard to keep their building expenses low from the start. They then need to leverage expensive residences to earn back their money paid to contractors and laborers.

The housing crisis in the U.S.

Let's take a closer look at one country's housing crisis: The United States.

In a study done by the National Association of Realtors (NAR), 87% of people said homeownership is part of the American Dream, and yet nearly 150 million Americans will likely never own their own home. That dream, for a substantial segment of the population, is an improbability.

The primary cause is the imbalance between home costs and average wages. When you look at the aggregate of Americans,

50% have a credit score that disqualifies them from getting a mortgage. Even more shocking is that 51% of people make less than $30K per year, and 91% of 100 U.S. cities have seen a recent increase in rent. Even those who are self-starters and highly-motivated entrepreneurs (like the 30% of Americans who are self-employed) are disqualified from mortgages.

It is difficult to get a mortgage based on credit approval, even if you save up your wages. The average U.S. rent is $12,600 per year ($1,050 per month). The average house down payment in 2018 was $14K. For someone who is scraping by with only twice that down payment as an annual salary, how long will it take them to pass this first bar of entry into homeownership? Especially when you factor in that nearly the exact same amount is paid on rent each year?

More than 38 million households have housing cost burdens, which means they pay more than 30% of their income on rent. It's no surprise that homeownership in America is at a five-decade low.

The American Dream of homeownership fell by the wayside for many following the 2008 housing crisis and the rise of crippling student loan debt. Even those who want to buy cannot, and 76% of young renters believed that homeownership makes more financial sense than renting.[5] In fact, in 2020, buying was more affordable than renting in about 64% of U.S. housing markets.[6]

It's not just poor people in cities who are struggling, and it's

---

[5] Fannie Mae

[6] Property Management

not just a problem of homeownership. Many middle-income Americans are finding it hard to afford rent, too. Almost 56% of renters earning $30,000 to $45,000 are also cost burdened. [7] The reasons are the same—the cost of rent is increasing at a pace faster than income.

When did renting and owning a home in the U.S. become impossible?

How is a person going to save up $14K for a down payment when they are paying over $12K in rent, especially if they're making less than $30K per year? The answer is they can't. Nearly half of their annual wages go to rent, and the rest may go to utilities, food, car payments, health care, children/schooling, childcare, and debt.

The impact on families

At the end of the day, we have to remember that we aren't just talking about numbers and statistics here. We're talking about real people—real families—with lived experiences. An unstable home, or unstable family unit, creates a chain reaction.

Take this story of Guillermo Galindo, reported by NPR (National Public Radio). In 2005, Galindo purchased a home in Massachusetts. He, his wife, and their newborn daughter lived downstairs and rented the upstairs unit. Galindo delivered medical supplies, and with the rent coming from the upstairs unit, their situation felt stable.

When his employer started cutting his hours after the 2008 crisis, and his interest rates on his mortgage started to rise, things

---

[7] Joint Center for Housing Studies of Harvard University

no longer felt stable. They took a turn for the worse when his upstairs tenants—a young mother and her baby, who were recently abandoned by the father—stopped paying.

Not wanting to kick the mother out while she was struggling, Galindo tried to make the mortgage payment on his own. He talked to the bank to see if they could make an arrangement. The value of his home had lost 50% of its original value in the current market. Selling wasn't going to bail Galindo and his family out of this situation.

The bank said they couldn't do anything for him and his family. Suddenly, the asset he'd hoped would be a long-term security for his family's well-being and their savings was a burden.

"I thought I was going to pass [the house] on to my daughter. I thought it was going to be something that would last for my remaining life."

The bank eventually sent him a foreclosure letter. Galindo handed over his keys. "It was very depressing for me," he said. "I was trying to show my best fact to my wife and my daughter. I remember we had a dog that was one of the things I promised my daughter if we had our own house…and it was really, really, really heartbreaking for me to find the words to tell my little one, who was probably three years old by then, that we were going to have to get rid of the dog. So, believe it or not, I wasn't even thinking about anything else but that how we were going to tell her that her dog was going to have to go."

Galindo and his family moved to an apartment where they ran a daycare facility out of their daughter's room by day and converted it to her bedroom by night. With a low credit score and no money saved up for a down payment, it would be a long time before they might afford a house again.

A home provides more than shelter

Homes provide security, control, belonging, identity, and privacy. But most of all, it's a place that provides us with a centering—a place from which we leave each morning and to which we return each evening. Children of homeowners do better in school (with higher test scores and lower antisocial behavior), and experience lower crime and drug usage. Compared to renters, homeowners are more likely to be involved in their communities through civic engagement, local elections, and volunteer work. Health outcomes are also better for homeowners.

The longer a person remains homeless, the more difficult it is to return to the mainstream of society. Being homeless is destabilizing, demoralizing, and depressing. Renting never feels like home, and the anxiety it can cause is immense. You never know when your housing situation might be taken from you, and you're always at the mercy of your landlord. You don't feel you can be part of the community, as you never know when you might have to go. The more you put in, the more upset you are to lose it.

Living in an owned home feels different from living in a rented home. It's not just that an owner can personalize the space; it touches a chord even more fundamental than that.

Homeownership enhances the longing for self-determination. First-time homeowners, young or old, radiate not only pride but also a sense of arrival, a sense of being where they belong. It cannot be duplicated by owning a ninety-nine-year lease.

Let's take a step-by-step look at how the pain, stress, and dysfunction of unstable housing radiates outward.

Let's say that John and Ana meet and fall deeply in love. They get married, live in a tiny apartment, work their 9-to-5 jobs, and scrape every penny for a down payment on a home with the dream of having a family.

They eventually have two children, and because of their steady wages, credit score, and down payment, they get approved for a home loan. They have made many sacrifices over the years: cutting coupons, shopping sales, saying "no" to wants that were not needs, and refraining from family vacations. They find an older house in a decent neighborhood within their budget, and they are happy to see that they are zoned for a pretty good school. After years of sacrificing, their dream is finally coming to fruition.

Things go well for a while, and they enjoy adding the finishing touches to their house. Since they are no longer in an apartment, they can tend to a yard on the weekends. Ana particularly enjoys selecting flowers for their landscaping and paint colors for the walls. John is still mindful of their budget, but they always make their mortgage payments on time.

One day at work, John is called into his supervisor's office to learn that the company is cutting 10% across the board, and he, unfortunately, is let go. As the primary breadwinner, John knows that this is detrimental to his family. This unforeseen situation is going to derail their dream. He realizes it will take a bit of time and paperwork to apply for unemployment compensation benefits and to locate a new job. Unfortunately for the couple, their savings went into the massive down payment for their home, and they had not yet built up their emergency fund account.

No one saw this coming.

John breaks the news to Ana who panics but then starts helping him search for jobs. The two tighten their purse strings and manage to pay one more month of their mortgage. When John contacts his bank to inform them of the situation, he learns that he and his family are nothing more than a number. They are told that if they cannot pay, they will go into default and their house will be foreclosed.

This couple, who did everything right, had one bump in the road, and lost the dream that they spent years working towards.

So, what happens next?

Theoretically, they have to sell. The house was a valuable asset. They had expected to sell it at an appreciated value and secure money for retirement, and maybe the kids' college fund. But given their need to sell quickly, the market is down, and they end up settling with the bank, with nothing left over.

John, Ana, and their two kids have to rent. They pay an application fee, a security deposit, and the first and last month's rent, and it nearly demolishes their savings. They are now in a tiny two-bedroom place. The kids have had to switch schools and John feels that as a provider to his family, he has failed. They know that if John cannot find lucrative employment, they are going to miss an upcoming rent payment and run the risk of being evicted. If that happens, they will have to move in with Ana's aging parents.

And all the while, the children are affected. One is quiet and withdrawn, and the other is yelling, fighting, getting into trouble at school, and neither John nor Ana have the capacity to provide their children with the extra care and reassurance that they need during this time. They wish they could hire an advisor to help them as a family, but it isn't possible. All they can do is prioritize and put one foot in front of the other.

Unfortunately, there are many real-life stories like this. Life is unpredictable. Most people don't have the safety net of a privileged family with additional resources. Some families take care of multiple family members who've struggled to thrive in modern society. I've heard stories from people who lost their homes, and have been in and out of homelessness because of unforgiving landlords, or landlords who change their mind. Some of these people cared for parents being treated for cancer, or children with additional needs. They aren't bad people in any way. They just found themselves in impossible situations. Some of them tell me, "I never thought this would happen to me."

Even someone who feels safe and secure in their job isn't immune to the unexpected. And there's nothing quite so terrible as being kept from a stable, safe home in which to care for and raise your family.

The pride of ownership

It could be assumed and agreed upon that a large majority of people will take care of, improve upon, invest in, and actually care for the condition of a home they own over a home they are simply renting. I call this the "pride of ownership."

When someone owns something, they feel better about it and try harder to maintain its quality. The majority of humanity will put blood, sweat, and tears into something that is theirs versus something that they are merely "borrowing."

Pride of ownership can be demonstrated and measured in different ways. The current subject is homes, but this can apply to nearly everything. Remember how you cared for your first car? Your first pet? You were so proud of it that you put in the necessary time and care to make sure your car looked nice and ran well, and that your pet was fed and cared for.

This pride of ownership is not always measured by how much money is invested in a home. Improvements can be made, such as good old-fashioned yard work on the weekends, cleaning up the gutters, sweeping the driveway or porch, or keeping the garage neat and tidy.

When something is yours, it is representative of the time, work, money, and sacrifices you have made to obtain it. It's worth the extra effort for the pride of ownership.

Of all the things that we as humans can own, the home is our most monumental possession. The home is our largest purchase, our biggest investment.

A home really is a place of memories and true happiness. This comes from creating experiences that will last forever, and a home is at the center of it all.

Homeownership versus renting

Typically, if homebuyers can afford a home, it is a wiser financial decision than renting. The house will most likely appreciate over time, which will build equity in the long run. Homeownership provides wealth. According to the Federal Reserve's Survey of Consumer Finances in 2013, a typical homeowner's net worth was $195,000, whereas a renter's net worth was $5,400. We can only assume those numbers are higher today.

Within the course of their lifetime, a homeowner will financially surpass a renter by a multiple of 45 on a financial achievement scale, which is based on median incomes. (Median income is used instead of mean income because, by eliminating the numerical influence of the ultra-wealthy, it more accurately represents the average person.)

Homeownership doesn't just benefit that individual family, but the economy at large. A typical homeowner buys multiple houses over the course of their life. In the process of selling and buying, they support the local economy. Whether it's hiring contractors for bathroom updates, professional cleaners, landscapers, or movers, or purchasing new furniture and appliances, NAR calculates that one new job is supported in the sale of every two homes. When someone can afford a home and the local cost of living, they also contribute to the economy as a consumer. A cost-burdened renter is less likely to support local coffee shops, mechanics, or retail stores.

Finally, children's futures are impacted by their parent's homeownership. The Boston Federal Reserve found that the income of homeowner's children rises as their home value rises. Generational wealth is a powerful indicator of future financial solvency for offspring. What we do in our life matters for future generations.

Let's look at the other side of the coin. Let's look at the family who rents.

Here, there is no pride of ownership. If something breaks, unless it is a major appliance, it's easy to envision the renter allowing a laundry list of fixes and small issues to pile up before taking them to their landlord. Things may be broken for a long time; lightbulbs burn out, cracks start to appear in walls or floors, grout splits apart, and sinks are slow to drain.

Since this house does not belong to them, there is no sense of urgency, no reason to spend their time or money on the house.

They are just renters. Do you think they will be in the yard pulling weeds, laying down mulch, or planting flowers on the weekend? Renters have zero reason to be invested in the property because they're merely borrowing it.

By having a landlord, families may feel less secure and more anxious. Even if they are good tenants, they are not in control of their destiny. Not everyone ends up in a rent-controlled apartment, and rent spikes can occur. Even if everything goes right, the burden of renting costs is high, forcing many families to pay more than 50% of their income. Unfortunately, these can price some families out of the property.

Other times, just one significant, unplanned expense, or the abrupt termination of a job, can make the difference between living in a home and being evicted. Take the story of Milton Light, an Arkansas resident, whose story was reported by NBC News.

Light worked as a coiled tubing operator. When he lost his job and was unable to pay rent, Light and his four children, with whom he shared custody with his ex-wife, suffered terrible harassment from his landlord. The landlord showed the home to new tenants, hired a moving truck to remove his possessions, tried to have his vehicle towed, turned off gas and electricity, and even called Human Services to claim that his home was unsafe for his children.

She didn't follow the proper eviction laws in the area, and tried to intimidate, bully, and remove Light from his home. Both sides filed lawsuits against the other, drawing out this unfortunate series of events. Amidst all of this, Light would have been trying to find a new job and provide for his family, all while worrying about what his landlord would do next, and whether he would have a place to return to.

This difficult situation happens far too often. People find themselves in challenging circumstances and are left with few options. Landlords might start showing houses to other people, change the locks, have the renter's possessions moved to the street, or call the police.

This isn't to be judgmental of landlords. Sometimes they also don't have a financial buffer, and the need to make a mortgage payment overpowers other options. Sometimes the lease agreement gives them the right to take action. Other times, this is simply how they conduct business. They want to be profitable. But there are ways to be profitable and also compassionate towards the uncertainty of life.

Can you imagine how it would feel if a landlord had little to no vested interest in your family, and at any point you might be on the street looking for other accommodations? How would that affect your family?

When a family owns rather than rents, they feel more in control. They have a pride of ownership, and their property will be cared for and will flourish. Owning their home, a family will remain in the neighborhood longer and become a valued part of a community.

The impact of homeownership on communities

Families are asking for help, and there are thousands of foreclosed homes that the banks cannot manage. The banks exist to open accounts and offer loans, not to serve as property managers. As a result, there are tens of thousands of abandoned homes that aren't being cared for and aren't housing someone in need.

Earlier I addressed the law of betterment with a hypothetical story of someone who owns a car that is old, broken, and not functioning properly. Along those same lines, if there are thousands of homes in a community with no electricity, receiving no care, and falling into disrepair, what impact does that have on the community at large? The houses around them are going to lose value. The community will be less desirable. The home may be targeted for crime, break-ins, graffiti, or other types of abuse. Safety in the area will be questioned.

If this happens to more than one home, these abandoned, foreclosed properties will cause people to choose other places to live. And the community will begin looking like a ghost town.

On top of the lowering aesthetics and decrease in value, there are other financial consequences. The state isn't getting property taxes. For each home that goes into foreclosure, communities receive less money for necessary services. As the value of the homes depreciates, the roads, schools, and public services receive less financial support. Local property taxes are increased to compensate for the decreasing quality. Those who can no longer afford the area have to leave, and those who can afford it won't want to live there.

On the other hand, if families are able to own their homes and put down roots, communities flourish. If John and Ana had been able to stay in their dream home, their children would have started succeeding in school with a regular circle of friends that progressed with them from grade to grade. They would have played sports, gained confidence, and felt stable enough to just be kids. John would have felt like a provider, and loved the home that he and Ana created together. She would have had several friends in the neighborhood, and they would have supported each other when someone was sick, needed a babysitter, a house sitter, a pet sitter, or an extra cup of sugar. The entire neighborhood would have been more stable and successful because this family flourished.

It's comfortable to go to the same market week after week, where you become friends with the person who bakes your bread, or provides your meat, or is your favorite cashier. It's comforting to bump into friends and neighbors at the park or the post office. A community provides familiarity and trust, and its residents enjoy a deeper level of life as a result.

To succeed and thrive as mankind, we need to have close-knit communities that trust us and know us. At the heart of it all is family, both biological and chosen.

Great things can be accomplished because of the security and certainty that comes with the family unit, and a stable community.

Current solutions

When it comes to the housing crisis, there's a sense of urgency. This problem isn't going away on its own. If anything, as the global population increases, and as more people migrate to cities, unaffordable housing and homelessness are only going to worsen.

In 2018, over 850 million people lived in informal settlements, a number that was predicted to grow to a billion within a couple of years.[8] However, the situation is not hopeless. I believe life gives back what you put in. And a lot of people are putting their

---

[8] Bloomberg CityLab

energy towards addressing this problem, including governments, educational institutions, and the private sector.

Berlin enacted a universal rent cap; some U.S. cities have created inclusionary zoning so that more land can be used for residences; British Columbia started taxing foreign real estate owners; universities are offering ethical design courses so they can approach home designing differently; and architects are partnering with engineers to manufacture low-cost building materials.

As with any complicated challenge, approaching solutions from different angles is an important strategy. A variety of players are putting their best ideas forward. But there's another angle, one that bypasses the red tape of industries and governments; one that involves us investors directly.

The UN stated in a report that if even a portion of the current global housing investments were "directed towards affordable housing and access to credit for people in need of it...adequate housing for all by 2030 would be well within reach."

As investors, we have the power to influence and shape the world. We can direct resources, and whether they seem large or small, every bit adds up.

We can contribute meaningfully to housing crisis solutions.

It all starts with a mindset shift. We need to change how we see real estate investments, from financial instruments to vehicles for impacting basic human rights.

Who's actually winning?

Obviously, the housing crisis has a widespread impact. It's impacting families, physical homes, land prices, communities, countries, and the world. But someone has to be winning in this system, or else it wouldn't flourish. Who's coming out on top?

The answer is people lending the money.

Banks are one of the most powerful institutions in this world. They have toppled governments and raised nations, and impact a great deal of modern life in many countries.

Banks primarily do two things: they hold money, and they lend money. But it's in lending where the banks make their real profit.

When it comes to lending, banks are in every facet of society. Lending is the bedrock that supports the industry of home buying and home improvements, car buying, college, agriculture, rentals, startup businesses, growing businesses, medicine, tourism, hotels, development, and so much more. All of these major industries are what they are today because of bank lending. And regardless of how much money these industries make, the banks are right there, making more.

If you're borrowing money, someone is profiting off of your hard work.

Even investors don't win against the bank

Let's say we have an investor named Tom. He puts 10% down on a house that costs $300K. Once Tom makes his initial down payment, he realizes that in order to increase the appeal of his property for a renter or buyer, it needs some work. He allocates another $50K to home improvements and updates. Tom is hoping that he can eventually raise the asking price for the house to cover the costs of renovations and make a profit of $50K.

How much time is Tom spending to make $50K? He is

looking at appliances and paying for countertops, paints, and floorings. He is meeting with designers and contractors. He's on the phone throughout his lunch breaks and evenings. He's at home improvement stores every weekend.

Tom just created another job for himself.

As Tom spends time, money, and energy on this property, who collects the interest? The bank. Tom is hoping that the property value will increase. But depending on the housing market, the value can conversely decrease.

If the market takes a dip and Tom's property loses value, this investor is essentially working for the bank. All the time spent on weekends improving this property begs the question: how valuable is Tom's time? What amount of money per hour is he actually making? If he were to calculate time spent versus profit earned, he would be shocked.

You can always earn more money, but you will never get back lost time.

So clearly, Tom is not the winner in this scenario. But there is a clear-cut winner, the recipient of effortless profit with nearly zero effort: the bank. Why? Consider this: If Tom made this property his job and paid off the bank ahead of schedule, then he'd be in a mediocre situation at best. But if Tom wants to hold the property long-term, and the housing market eventually takes a hit, what happens then? Tom's property value goes below what he owes the bank, and either he keeps paying the bank their interest, or the bank repossesses the house.

Bank 1, Tom 0.

The #1 player in the real estate world is banks.

Real estate is a numbers game

Something banks don't want real estate investors to know is that they work the numbers. They model how many people will make their payments, and how many won't. They rarely ever find themselves in dire situations. How many times have you heard of a bank going bankrupt? It's much rarer than any other type of business, right? For banks, their lending model almost always makes financial sense.

If we analyze the entire real estate industry in 2019 and 2020, on average, 50,000 properties foreclosed every month. That means the banks collected monthly income from those properties for however many years the homeowner could make the payment, and they still ended up with the asset of the house. Let's say that before foreclosure, some of these homeowners paid their mortgage for up to five, six, or even seven years. All of that was money received at no cost for the banks.

Now, the bank has the property again. They will put it back on the market, likely selling it as a fix-and-flip, without doing any of the work to improve the property. And where does the investor turn for a loan to execute that fix-and-flip? The bank.

The bank received interest payments from the homeowner, then from the investor who's flipping it, and possibly from the new home buyer. The bank makes money again and again. Multiply that by hundreds of thousands of homes, and their business model looks genius. They're making most of the money without doing any of the heavy lifting.

One of the crucial things about the bank's game is they do not put all of their money in one basket. They lend to multiple people, diversifying their strategy. It's a game of averages. If you make 15% per loan, and lend to one person, your investment lives or dies by that one person: either 0% or 15%. When you lend to 10 people, and 70% of the people pay as they should, then you have made a 10% return on all of your money, including the people who didn't pay. This is how banks can trust the process of giving away money through loans.

The banks have their numbers down to a science.

Banks benefit off homeowners

Let's zoom in on an example to personalize this. It has been remarked in the housing industry that an American will move 11.4 times on average in their lifetime.

Carlos will live an average of seventy to seventy-five years. Carlos bought his first home between the ages of twenty to twenty-five. It was small and modest, yet cozy. (Gone are the days where someone's first or second home is their "forever home.")

Carlos is chasing the American Dream and will pursue gradually bigger properties, relocate for better job opportunities, will keep school zones in mind (and may move because of one), and will make other similar considerations. Once Carlos' kids are out of the house, he may move closer to where his son attends college, or he may move closer to act as a caregiver for his parents, or he may relocate to live near his daughter, who has just had his first grandchild.

If we take the average of moving eleven times over a period of 50 years, Carlos will be moving roughly every five years. So how does the bank perceive this long, full life?

The bank knows that when they first meet Carlos, he will be

going into debt for his home. The bank tells Carlos, "Absolutely, we'll give you $300K for your dream home."

After a handshake and a smile, they know that in five to seven years, Carlos will try to get rid of that initial home. If he encounters financial hardship, or if Carlos needs to move, the home will be back in the hands of the bank. From the bank's perspective, Carlos's mortgage loan is a safe investment.

In a shocking report by RealtyTrac in 2018, U.S. bank repossessions cost nearly 60,000 families to lose their homes in one month of the year. That level of loss continues even today in 2020, averaging 40,000 families a month in the last fifteen years. That is not just 40,000 people; a family is usually two adults, some children, perhaps a grandparent…Let's just say for all intents and purposes, that each home houses, on average, four individuals. That means that 160,000 people are directly affected and impacted by a bank repossessing their house every single month. A ripple effect is felt in their extended family, neighborhoods, schools, and communities.

What if you could be the bank, with a special touch?

When it comes to the housing investor who ends up with the glorified title of 'landlord', well, simply put, being the bank in the housing industry is much better than being the landlord. It isn't exclusive to the landlord, either. It's much better to be the bank than the homebuyer, or the fixer and flipper. You get the picture—the bank always wins.

If you want to be an investor, know that the number one player in this game is the bank, not the landlord.

It makes you want to rethink everything, doesn't it? Good thing we've created a new process for you! Because the Housing

PhilanthroInvesting model is all about the question: how do you become a bank that cares about hard-working families who also want to contribute to life?

Be the bank

As an entrepreneur with a vested interest in the real estate industry, I found this information to be truly enlightening. The traditional real estate system has many flaws for an investor looking to grow their personal capital and increase their cash flow.

The bank's example was useful and instructive. I realized that, in order to be a Housing PhilanthroInvestor, I needed to combine the fixer and flipper, and the bank business model, and create a turnkey business model. You will understand what I mean in the next chapter.

There are three possible outcomes when lending money and caring about hard-working families with good intentions. Each of them favors the lender:

1. The borrowers either do not pay and you, as the bank, get the asset back to resell and profit from.
2. The borrowers pay off the loan to their bank (in this case, you) when they find a more favorable option for borrowing money (and you as the bank make all of your money back, plus equity).
3. The borrower pays off the loan in the agreed-upon way, and you as the bank get all of your money back, plus profit.

Whichever way, the bank benefits. That is real stability against recession because your investment is backed by a physical asset.

Being the lender also frees you up to operate in multiple geographical areas. The main difference between the lender and the landlord is that the lender isn't really responsible for tending to the home—the landlord is. When you are a lender, geography matters much less. Many banks lend money for properties outside their geographic area, unless they are strictly local banks.

But the best part of being the lender is that you get to decide to whom you extend a loan, and what the circumstances of that loan will be.

When you're the bank, you change the game for homeowners

If investors, bankers, and lenders acted in accordance with the law of betterment, we would see progress in the global housing crisis.

Imagine if there was a change to how loans operated, a change in the heart of investors, bankers, and lenders, putting the best interest of a community first.

If a family has a medical emergency, instead of the bank saying, "If you don't send your payment, you will default on your mortgage, and your home will go into foreclosure," they would say something more understanding and forgiving, like, "Okay, if you could please send proof of your medical emergency, and upon approval, we can provide an additional thirty or sixty days to pay, or possibly gift you that payment if you show that you have added value to your home, or to a neighbor's home."

Wow! That's a game changer.

This isn't a new concept. After hurricanes and other natural disasters, companies are more than willing to step up and offer extensions on payments. They do this as a marketing action to say, "Look at us, we're helping during a disaster, we're the best." It's usually done to get better visibility, more clients, and more money. Unfortunately, they only extend this gesture when it benefits them.

But if this concept became the norm—if banks started looking at people as families instead of just numbers—they would be helping the communities at large. They would understand that sometimes life happens and flexibility is required. They would realize that this is good business practice.

This is another benefit of you becoming the bank. As a PhilanthroInvestor who cares about the well-being of the planet, you get to make the rules for your homeowners. You can create a new way of operating that supports people first, finances second. You can be flexible with their needs, ensuring that they stay in their homes when times are rough and they need it most.

As a society, we have created a system that is out of balance. Families cannot afford homes. People earning only $30K a year can barely make their $12K annual rent payment, thus leaving them with no way to save up the necessary $14K for a down payment. It's a vicious cycle.

Because we've contributed to the problem, we as a society are responsible for fixing it.

By transferring your money and time previously devoted to Wall Street, and dedicating it to Your Street, we generate kindness, support, and goodwill.

As Housing PhilanthroInvestors, we send a message to the banks and lenders that there are other ways to handle real estate when a family is in need. We send the message that kicking a family out of their home is detrimental to society, works against the law of betterment, and negatively impacts the planet.

The way to achieve a thriving society is through enabling a stable family unit by getting families in homes and keeping them there.

Take a Moment to PhilanthroInvest

What was your household like growing up? Were you raised in the same stable home? How has that affected where you are today?

_____

_____

_____

_____

_____

Can you think of someone in your life who experienced an unstable family unit or home? What do you remember about this friend, classmate, or family member?

_____

_____

_____

_____

_____

Do you see the value in supporting family units by providing them with stable homes? If you were able to help a family in need, like the example with John and Ana, while growing your capital, would you?

_____

_____

_____

_____

_____

If homeownership and rent costs continue increasing at a higher rate than income, and every family pays retail cost, what will our world look like in five years, or ten?

_____

_____

_____

_____

_____

How will marriages, workplaces, schools, and children be affected if a family is frequently moving, starting over, and living in unstable conditions? How will that affect neighborhoods, communities, cities, states, the nation, and _you?_

_____

_____

_____

_____

_____

Have you or someone you know experienced an unexpected situation that affected their ability to pay bills (even temporarily)? Was there a new baby, a medical expense, a glitch in paychecks, anything that prevented you or that person from meeting a financial responsibility?

_____

_____

_____

_____

Knowing that there is a more understanding, kind, and humane way to handle family living situations, do you feel called to be a part of the movement to elevate society through stabilizing families?

_____

_____

_____

_____

Have you ever worn the lender hat before? Knowing what you now know about the power of banks, do you see how this role could benefit you and meet your investing goals?

_____

_____

_____

_____

Chapter 6
PhilanthroInvesting and Housing

How PhilanthroInvesting helps homeowners

Now that you know the importance of help, a stable family unit, and the pride of ownership, I would like to share with you how we can save neighborhoods while strengthening your housing portfolio. It happens through the power of The HappyHome Triangle.

In this model, the top corner is the HappyHome. The lower corner on the left represents the PhilanthroInvestor, and on the right is the family.

This visual essentially demonstrates the goal of Housing PhilanthroInvesting, which is three-fold:

1. Investing with a purpose while generating a return.
2. Keeping families in their homes.
3. Increasing the value of a house through diligent care to save neighborhoods, one home at a time.

As you'll see in the eight-step process we're going to explore next, there's a unique component to the HappyHome triangle. Although we're helping families have the opportunity to become homeowners, they don't simply passively occupy their homes. A HappyHome is created through an active process of bettering the house itself. This even becomes part of the screening process for families with whom you work as a PhilanthroInvestor—you want to find families who are eager to display their pride of ownership by investing in their home. Whether through improving the shingle-siding, repainting, or landscaping, these families are integral to completing the HappyHome triangle.

The more PhilanthroInvestors participate in this model, the more families will be helped, and the more homes will be improved, resulting in better neighborhoods. Every time we shift resources away from the current global housing retail market, or the stock market, or the gambling and speculation markets, we contribute towards a solution. We write a new narrative for the state of the world. We leave a legacy for future generations that we can be proud of.

Spreading the wealth—Housing PhilanthroInvesting

I would like to stipulate that I am not a lawyer, and when it comes to protecting your assets, you should seek legal counsel.

However, having managed over $30 million in real estate,

developed this model with care, and facilitated many Housing PhilanthroInvestors transactions, I'm honored to share my process with you.

It is possible to do Housing PhilanthroInvesting on your own, which is what I'm going to teach you in this book. To be fully transparent, we also have services that can do this in a joint venture with you, which I'll touch on briefly near the end of the book. However, if you choose to be autonomous in your PhilanthroInvesting role, I couldn't be more supportive. The world is abundant. If billions of families are helped because of this vision and this process, then I've done my job. My purpose is to create new games in the world of investing so that, together, we can shape a different kind of world, while reaching true financial freedom for all.

At the end of the book, there are notes about resources online where you can learn more. I'm going to give you the broad overview, but should you choose to PhilanthroInvest, your knowledge should go beyond this book. Feel free to dive into those resources, and an online course with all the appropriate templates, so that you can confidently wear your Housing PhilanthroInvestor hat, knowing you can control all of the particles.

Housing PhilanthroInvesting combines the trader, the enhancer, the lender, and the holder hats.

Housing PhilanthroInvesting solves one of the primary problems of the housing crisis: the accessibility issue.

It requires multiple hats. A Housing PhilanthroInvestor finds or builds homes under market value, and might do some basic enhancing. Then, they trade that home for more than their total investment, but still below market value. By becoming the bank, they position themselves as the ultimate lender, holding the asset long-term, and lending the home to a family while maintaining the physical asset. The house is also backed by the hard-working, good-intentioned family unit which occupies and improves the house. This is how we can shift the planet in a more positive direction.

The amazing thing about combining these hats in housing is that you receive profit cash flow and capital cash flow from every payment. You don't need to wait to recover your money in order to grow your assets. They both start growing on day one when you receive your first payment of principal and interest. With any loan on a house, the first half of the payments will be primarily interest, and the latter half will be primarily principal.

The lender is the only hat that earns interest. The word "interest" in Latin means "it is important." When a lender lends an asset that is important to someone else, the lender earns money on top of the principal capital investment. In the end, you're paid even more cash in exchange for that asset. The way I see it, by helping a family achieve something important, you are paid cash (including both capital and profit cash flow) in regular installments.

When you wear the lender hat, you start winning right away.

Eight steps for saving neighborhoods

I've broken down the process of Housing PhilanthroInvesting into eight steps. This is a process you can do once, or repeat with multiple families across multiple properties. Personally, I would recommend doing numerous. As we learned from the banks, there is a numbers element to successful housing investing. If you just have one investment, then all your eggs are in one basket. If you have a few, your results can balance each other out.

This is also a model you can replicate in multiple places. It is not geographic dependent. However, I would suggest starting locally. For one thing, you will really feel the benefits of the laws of betterment and giving back knowing you're improving the community ecosystem right in your city. It will also be easier to manage the transactions if the families are close, especially when you're just starting out.

The last consideration I'll leave you with is this: although I'm going to give you a framework, which is a turnkey business that has proven to work for almost a decade now, just remember that it's important to consult a lawyer about any and all PhilanthroInvesting activity. You want to protect yourself and your assets and abide by the law of your land. That way, if something were to go wrong, your future is not at risk.

I suggest running your turnkey business using a company that you control. Check with your lawyer to determine the best type of company in your own country.

The eight steps we will be exploring are:

1. Create a trust
2. Buy or build a home
3. Basic repairs (when buying a home)
4. Create a seller financing agreement
5. Find a qualified family
6. Onboard the family and create a HappyHome
7. Work with issues that arise
8. Do it again!

Step #1: Create a trust

The first step is to create a legal protection entity specific to this asset. One way to do this is by creating a specific purpose trust, or in some countries, a land trust.

A trust, in legal terms, is any arrangement in which one party holds property for another party's benefit. You can create a specific purpose trust for almost anything, including cars, inheritance, and of course land.

Your trust will purchase the house that will be used in your PhilanthroInvesting deal. The best kept secret of multi-million-dollar investors is that you can own hundreds or thousands of properties, and put each of those into individual trusts while naming someone else as your trustee, such as a family, friend, or another trusted person. Ideally, you want someone with property management experience. The trustee becomes the manager of the asset, and the responsible party for the property.

Trusts also provide shelter by granting you anonymity and creating a buffer between you and buyers, regulations, and local governments.

You can share the trust with another if you so choose (say you have another investor with whom you're PhilanthroInvesting). You both can be beneficiaries of the trust, with a 50% ownership split.

When it comes to the land trust itself, you can dictate what happens. I want to drive this point home. With this privacy strategy, you can "own nothing," but control everything. The privacy that's offered to beneficiaries exists in most of the countries of the world where I have researched trusts.

Step #2: Buy or build a home

The next step is to find and buy a house, or build one. You want to find undervalued houses so that you can purchase something below market value. This will be critical for actually being able to PhilanthroInvest. Yes, you want to make a profit, but not at the expense of a family's well-being.

The best place to look for homes is at real estate auctions. Often, these will be foreclosed houses or homes owned by banks. Banks weren't made to manage properties; they merely want to retrieve their investment. Houses being sold at auction are often below the market value for that area.

As you consider the homes for sale, here are a few things to ask yourself:

- Is this an area in which a family can earn enough to make loan payments?
- Are there tenants who want to be homeowners in this area?
- What is the ratio of homeowners to tenants? (The more tenants there are, the greater your potential to do Housing PhilanthroInvesting.)
- Is the crime rate low in this neighborhood? (We want our families to be safe in their HappyHome.)
- Is there accessibility to services and jobs close to the home? Can families get to work on a bus, or shop for food and get medical attention? (This entire infrastructure will support your families.)
- Is this generally an area where people want to live, especially for its location?

Once you find a home that fits the above requirements, and you know you can purchase it below the market value so that you can benefit a family while earning reasonable interest, purchase the home through your trust in cash. Remember, part of the path to true financial freedom is to be debt-free. This model only works if you can own the property outright and work with the family, without the influence of a bank or another lender, unless you have a partner in the deal.

After you purchase your home, the first thing to do is purchase liability and hazard insurance with your trust as the beneficiary and protect your asset. (Remember from the seven basic factors of investing that every asset has inherent liability? This is how we protect ourselves against it!) If you're going to purchase multiple homes to PhilanthroInvest, negotiate your insurance rates with the company, because you're going to be working with them at scale.

As I highlighted above, there's another option: instead of purchasing a home, you can build a home. If you choose to do so, you must ensure you can build the home below the market value. You want to have an agreement with your contractor that lays out the cost of each step.

Let's say, between the lot and the construction, you build the home for $50K, and the value in that area is $100K. Then you can sell it to the family for $75K. That way, you will be getting a profit, plus interest, and the family is getting a deal compared to the market value. They essentially start out with $25K worth of equity on day one (that's the philanthropy of Philanthro-Investing).

Step #3: Basic repairs

When you buy a house at auction or a foreclosed house, you'll find that they've often been neglected, either by the previous owners, or the auction house. They're abandoned. They may

149

have trash, broken appliances, or odd things left behind, like a car or a boat, or jewelry.

The first thing to do is clean the house, and make it safe with basic repairs. Replace any broken windows, fix any exposed wires, or rotted floors. Make the home inhabitable and secure, but not necessarily beautiful. Leave the creativity part to the family who will enjoy deciding colors, flooring types, and appliances for their home.

Regarding material possessions left behind by previous owners, donate them to a local charity if they're useable, including the car or the boat. Some people might feel tempted to keep these things or sell them, but I would encourage you to remember your Purpose Line. What do you want to accomplish? Why do you do the things you do? If your intention is to help others, then you will continue to expand your Purpose Line by donating these items rather than finding ways to profit off them, which will also take time away from managing your Housing PhilanthroInvesting business. You will be profiting off of this home in a holistic way; don't spoil that intention by finding other ways to scrape up an income.

No matter what investor hat you wear, or what kind of PhilanthroInvesting you do, it's important to know what things are off your Purpose Line, so you can be aware of them. Now, if you can find a way to sell valuable items found in the home and put that money towards improving the home for the family, you're still within your Purpose Line. It all comes down to intent.

Finally, as you complete the repairs and clean the home, make sure to change all of the locks, and secure any windows or other entrances that need to be secured, depending on the area. You don't know who previously owned a key to this home, but you want to make sure only your family can get in going forward.

Step #4: Create a seller financing agreement

Before finding a family for your home, you want to know what your agreement will be so that you can find a qualified family.

A seller financing agreement is a document of terms that you will draw up with a lawyer. I am not a lawyer, nor am I giving you legal advice. You need to find someone who knows all about how to create this agreement to fit your local laws. They will also help you protect yourself and your asset in case the family isn't paying, or you need to proceed with eviction.

Here's how to accomplish it: ask the lawyer to create a template that you can use for all of your arrangements going forward. You'll only have to change the main information of the agreement, like the property address, the name of your trust, the name of the family, and the date of the deal. Also, ask your lawyer for their advice regarding protection. How can you have the highest protection for this transaction? Some countries require a notary to certify your signatures to make it legally binding. Some accept digital signatures. Others require a witness and some just a signature without notarization or witnesses. Ideally, your lawyers should provide written approval that the documents they drew up, and the operating basis they advised, abide by local laws.

There are a few basic things to consider as you create this document:

- Arrange it so that the trust maintains ownership of the deed until the family has completely paid off the home.
- I would recommend creating an agreement that lasts

twenty years.

- When determining the interest rate, it should be higher than inflation, and make sense for you to run a profitable business. Does double the annual inflation rate make sense? (Your interest rate will likely be higher than a bank; you are selling the home for lower than market price and passing the family equity, and making money through the interest rate.)
- In each monthly payment, the family should pay on the principal and interest, as well as taxes and home insurance. (They will pay you the latter two, and you will pay the insurance company and the property tax to the government, if required. Some governments do not charge property taxes.)
- You should be charging less each month than what they'd pay in rent in this area for that type of home size (number of bedrooms and bathrooms).
- The down payment should be no more than one month's worth of the average salary, and no lower than one month's minimum salary in the area.
- Include a clause that not only is the family responsible for paying the monthly loan payment (which includes principal, interest, taxes, and home insurance), they are also committed to creating a HappyHome, which includes maintaining and improving the asset (more about this in Step #6).
- Include a clause that highlights the very important fact that your trust is selling this home *as is*, and that the family has properly inspected it.

It's a bit of a balancing act finding the sweet spot for this home, its future family, and this agreement. Every transaction will be different, just as every local law will be different. In general, you want to sell the home for more than you paid to acquire it, but below the market value or after repair value (ARV), as it's called in some markets, so that this family can actually become homeowners. To help you calculate things like the monthly payments, I've included a reference at the end of the book that will take you to an online calculator.

Finally, later we will discuss another clause that should be included in the seller financing agreement, which is the abandonment clause. Even though we don't want things to go wrong in this transaction, it's important to plan for the worst-case scenario to ensure that you're protected.

Let's dive a little more deeply into how you can determine your ARV.

Determining ARV

The ARV is the price at which you sell the home after you have completed the basic repairs. In order to determine your ARV, you need to start by finding comparable homes in the area. Ideally, this would be the same neighborhood in which your home is located. Even one block can make a difference in home values.

In addition to the physical location, look for homes that are similar in square footage and amenities. This would include the number of bathrooms and bedrooms, the lot size, similar fixtures and finishings, and maybe even when the house was built. Also look for a home that was sold within the last three to six months, as that will more accurately reflect the current market.

The house you identify that meets these criteria is called a "comp," or a comparable home. If you can find three to five comps, it will help you determine the most accurate ARV.

From here, you can break down the analysis even further. Given the selling amount of each comp, you can determine approximately how much each "feature" costs. For example, maybe a comp bedroom costs $10,000. If the comp has four bedrooms, and your property has two, you can quantify the difference by adding a negative value to the difference of bedrooms:

(−2 beds) x ($10,000) = −$20,000

In this process, you're building a model that will adjust the features in your home to the comp, arriving at an accurate ARV.

Once you've determined the value of features for the comp, and you've determined the difference to your property (that difference will be either positive or negative), you can adjust the sold price accordingly.

For example, if your property has two fewer bedrooms than the comp, but an additional bathroom, and all other features are equal, your final equation would be:

(−2 beds) x ($10,000) = −$20,000

(+1 bath) x ($5,000) = +$5,000

Adjusted value = −$15,000

Repeat this process with three to five comps until you have an adjusted value for each. Then, determine the square footage value of the home based on the adjusted value (adjusted value/comp square footage). Determine an average square footage value among all of the comps:

(Comp 1 + Comp 2 + Comp 3) ÷ 3

Then multiply that number by your home's square footage. This should give you the most accurate ARV for your home!

Step #5: Find a qualified family

Now that the house is ready, you've prepared an agreement with a lawyer and understand the terms, it's time to find a qualified family.

Place multiple large, colorful, attractive signs on the home that communicate things like "small down payment, no credit check, no banks, for sale by owner," and your phone number. These variables will attract the type of family you are looking for: unable to become homeowners using traditional bank financing, yet very capable of meeting your terms.

You can also advertise on local social media groups with your own social media profile, or in other strategic locations where people are looking for homes. You can also advertise where people look to rent. Include a statement that says they can become a homeowner for less than the cost of rent.

When interviewing families, you want literal proof (bank statements) that they make at least 4x the monthly payment. This will provide assurance that they can actually pay you. You also want recommendations from previous landlords, whom you can call to inquire about these tenants.

The final component of qualification is to ask if this family is do-it-yourselfers. They need to have a background in working on house projects, whether that has been a previous home in which they've lived, a family member's home, experience making a crib for a baby, or some other sign of interest in physical work.

In this process of PhilanthroInvesting, we are also guiding families in homeownership. We don't want them to be spending money on hired help to paint, or stain a deck, or landscape the yard. As you will soon find out, this family has an important agreement with you to do household projects, improving the asset for the law of betterment, for themselves, and also for their neighborhood. It's important to know this family can do weekend projects and will get value out of improving their home together!

Step #6: Onboarding the family and creating a HappyHome

Now is when the magic begins. When onboarding the family and delivering the keys, if you are physically in that city or state and you have the availability to do so, give yourself and the family a treat: get two stakes (ideally torches) and put a green ribbon between them. Have a few scissors, buy a small tree, and invite the family to their future HappyHome. When they come:

A. Light the torches.
B. Give the scissors to each parent, or a parent and a child, and invite them to cut the green ribbon while you take pictures.
C. Invite them to plant a tree in their future HappyHome and take pictures of it.

A HappyHome is a measurable, quantifiable variable that you get to create. After you complete the basic repairs, there will be other updates that can be made to the house. Maybe it's pulling off wallpaper and painting, or clearing overgrown plants, or updating tile in the bathroom. As the Housing PhilanthroInvestor, you create a checklist for what the homeowners can do to truly make this a HappyHome. The checklist is your standardized definition of a HappyHome, with items personalized to this house.

Part of your agreement with the family is that they will work on this checklist. As they complete projects, they will send you pictures. This process improves the value of your investment and increases their equity in the home. For an example HappyHome checklist, you can check out our online course referenced in the back of the book.

Once your family has completed all of the items on the checklist, you can reward them by covering their Christmas monthly payment. It makes for a thoughtful present, and is your way to encourage them, and thank them, for putting sweat equity into the house and for supporting the law of betterment.

Last but not less important, if you would like, please share the pictures that you collect of these moments with me through our social media channels. I would greatly appreciate it!

Step #7: Working with issues that arise

Even after executing steps 1 through 6 with meticulous care and attention, things can still go wrong. Families hit hard times, or you choose a family that wasn't the right fit. You need to have a protocol in place for different scenarios, so that you aren't left wondering how to proceed.

Two types of families

In my experience with Housing PhilanthroInvesting, there are two types of families: families with good intentions, and families with bad intentions. The majority of families, almost all of them, are good-intentioned families.

There is a basic way to determine if a family has good intentions or not: they are communicative. If a family is engaging with you, even as they encounter obstacles, that means they want to maintain their home and work towards homeownership. A good-intentioned family lets you know when they are struggling financially, and works with you to make a plan.

Bad-intentioned families ultimately seek to abuse the system. They are not a good fit for PhilanthroInvesting because they don't actually want to do what it takes to create a HappyHome. They won't communicate with you when challenges arise. They might miss payments without explanations.

It's important to have a protocol in place for these two scenarios.

When a good-intentioned family misses a payment

The nature of this kind of investing is generosity. You're providing options for those who otherwise would not have them. These are families that can't get loans from traditional banks and haven't been afforded the same opportunities as other homeowners. The philanthropy part of your role (the part that sold the home to them below the after repair value and passed potential equity to them) is supporting this family in the face of life's inevitable ups and downs.

It might be that this family is suffering from a medical emergency. Or maybe they need to help another family member who's fallen into difficulty. Or their employer is in transition, and they were let go. Whatever the situation, if a good-intentioned family misses a payment and they're communicating with you about it, you have a few options. This is one of the most phenomenal parts of Housing PhilanthroInvesting—through your creativity and desire to help, you can keep families in their homes, even when times get tough.

The following four options for how to handle late payments are predicated on the ability of the family to provide some kind of proof of their hurdle. Whether it's a bank statement to show you they simply don't have the money right now, a doctor's note, or an official notice of dismissal from their employer, you want physical proof to support their claim.

The first option: You can simply charge a late fee. This is the best path if the homeowner is only late a few days or weeks. If they're able to pay the missed payment in a relatively quick time, charge a small fixed late fee, so they have a reason for not being late (like $20 or $25, for example).

The second option: Leverage the HappyHome process to improve your asset. If your family has not finished their HappyHome checklist, agree upon the tasks you would like them to complete in lieu of their missed payment. This option has a little more philanthropy in it—you're offering to exchange their owed cash for labor as proof that they are supporting the natural law of betterment.

If the family has completed the HappyHome checklist, then you can get creative. Perhaps there's a neighbor close by with whom they have a relationship, or they can create a new relationship. Brief the family on what a stranger really is: a friend that we don't know yet. Remind them that all friends and most family members were strangers at some point in the past. They need to identify neighbors whose house requires some work, because remember, by the law of betterment, if the houses around theirs are improved, the condition and value of their house will also improve. In that case, have this family help that neighbor achieve a HappyHome with their labor (the family you are supporting is the only one allowed to do the work!). This also improves your asset by uplifting the value of the neighborhood as a whole. It also allows them to experience the spiritual benefit of helping others. Have the family send you pictures of their work, so you have proof of their efforts.

I would recommend only allowing this option once a year. However, the decision is entirely up to you. Perhaps you tell your family that for every neighboring home they uplift into a HappyHome, you will cover one month of their loan payment, or half. It's all about your comfort level, what you want to accomplish through this investment, and how much you want to be involved in improving the lives of homeowners and neighborhoods! This option should also be reviewed on a case-by-case basis. It will require more of your engagement, but it can be a rewarding process.

The third option: Refinance the home. You can add the amount that was missed (whether it was one month, or two months, or more) to the loan as a whole. For example, if the original loan was for $50,000, and the family missed two month's loan payments, which cost $1,000 in total, their new loan amount would be $51,000.

The family monthly payments will increase to reflect the new sum total paid over twenty years. The upside for you is that you'll make more than that $1,000 of monthly payments through the interest of the $1,000 over the years.

For some families, this option feels enticing, as it delays the need to pay anything right now. I would only deploy refinancing once every three to five years, to prevent over-reliance. But again, it is your decision as their PhilanthroInvestor.

The fourth option: Create an extension plan. Instead of fully refinancing the due amount into the principal of the loan, you can create an extension plan whereby the family pays the missing balance over the next few monthly payments. For example, if they miss three months, the next three months can be double. Or you can split the payments over six months, increasing each payment by half until they catch up on their loan.

You get to decide how involved you want to be, and how much philanthropy you want in your PhilanthroInvesting. If you have multiple homes and multiple families, you might want to review each situation individually. Still, it will be useful to have these options in your back pocket, so that you know how to guide the process of financial difficulty among good-intentioned families, all with the goal of keeping them in their homes, and supporting them in achieving the pride of ownership.

When a bad-intentioned family misses a payment

As I mentioned in Step #4, when creating the seller financing agreement, you want to include an abandonment clause. This clause states that if there is proof that the family has abandoned the home, the lender gets to reclaim it, and the family loses all rights. The abandonment clause serves to protect you in case a bad-intentioned family doesn't honor your agreement and leaves the house.

Abandonment is different from eviction. When a family leaves the home, it's abandonment; if the family refuses to pay and refuses to leave, you will need to call upon your local eviction laws to remove the family and reclaim the house.

Neither of these scenarios is something to take lightly. I realize it's not fun to think about, but you need to protect yourself and your asset. This is why the property deed remains under the trust until the last cent of the loan is paid back. This will give you the ability to take the home back if a family is non-communicative, or there is proof that they've abandoned the property.

As with all of the recommendations in this book, please consult a lawyer. They will know the local eviction laws, which are important to understand in this process.

When a family misses a payment and they have not reached out to let you know, the first step is to call them. See if you can get hold of them and learn what's going on. If you make contact, you can use any of the previous options for navigating repaying the missed payments.

If you don't hear back from the family, start sending letters in the mail telling them to be in contact with you. The third option is to go and visit the family yourself if you live in the area. If someone is home, this is another chance to engage with them about what is happening and work towards a solution. You always want to carry the benefit of the doubt and assume that this is a good-intentioned family.

If you don't hear back from the calls or the letters, and no one answers the door, it's time to start sending notifications. Each step in this process increases the level of justice, all while continuing to give the family opportunities to take responsibility for the situation. The notices are warnings to the family that if they don't get in contact with you and make a plan to pay you back, they are at risk of being evicted. Send a notice every day for ten days, and increase the saturation of the color, from yellow, to pink, to orange, to red.

Finally, if everything else has failed, call your local sheriff to visit the property with you. In parts of the world where the justice system is organized and honest, the sheriff/police are there to help you enforce the seller financing agreement, including stipulations about missed payments and a lack of communication. If there is evidence that the family has abandoned the home, your agreement will state that you can reclaim the home. If the family is there but refuses to pay or leave, work with your lawyer and the sheriff to proceed with the eviction process. Remember that the job of the good police system is law enforcement, and you have a right to seek their support.

Up until the point where you arrive with a sheriff, your goal is to convert this family into a good-intentioned family. They might be unfamiliar with this process, or they might be defaulting to old habits of avoiding authority figures when they encounter difficulty. Perhaps they haven't known previous lenders to be supportive, so they're protecting themselves by avoiding you. Some people have been badly betrayed in the past after someone said they would help. With kind communication, you might be able to reach past their fear of betrayal and find a way forward.

It's possible this family will still be interested in working with you to turn the situation around, and to remain on the path to HappyHome ownership. Keep that positive spirit alive. Assume the best, but protect yourself in your financing agreement should the worst happen.

Step #8: Do it again!

Housing PhilanthroInvesting is not just a one-time thing. It is a new way of investing with a purpose, and you as an investor have the opportunity to do it as much as you want.

In fact, there's a benefit to having a number of Housing PhilanthroInvestments. By owning multiple homes in a few different areas, you further mitigate the risk that one piece of property might bring (if, for example, the area becomes less desirable, or a large employer in the area goes out of business). Diversification across areas of the housing industry provides protection against instability in one area. Multiple homes, with different families, help you grow your wealth with lower risk.

Another benefit is you get to help even more families! With the current global housing crisis, we have a long way to go. When it comes to helping people own their homes and create their own legacy through asset ownership, the more HappyHomes we can facilitate, the greater dent we'll make. Be a benevolent bank, broaden your Purpose Line, and invest your money in things that matter.

Housing PhilanthroInvesting covers all of your needs

Housing PhilanthroInvesting is a path to true financial freedom. When you wear this hat, you will achieve: knowledge, engagement, purpose, control, cash flow, capital growth, enjoyment, fulfillment, and legacy. Here's a highlight of just four of these variables:

Good, consistent returns

With Housing PhilanthroInvesting, you combine multiple investors' hats and increase your net worth by enhancing a home with basic repairs and trading it for legal lending documents at a higher value in less than a year. Then, you use your lender hat and receive monthly payments that include capital and profit cash flow.

Low risk

You can be more confident than ever about the stability of your investment by choosing families who have income and free time for fixing up the property. You can also make your business recession-proof.

In the case of the 2008 real estate crash in the U.S., the crash on residential prices was 21%. If you acquire the homes and do the basic repairs and the total investment for you in that home ends up being lower than 21% below the market value, then you are protected even from the worse real estate crisis in history.

During the COVID-19 crisis, I learned something from our first Housing PhilanthroInvesting firm in the world, Equity & Help, Inc (www.equityandhelp.com), which as of today manages more than 400 families using the methodology you are learning in this book. The PhilanthroInvestors of Equity & Help felt quite good about being able to provide housing to essential workers, like nurses, firemen, plumbers, basic contractors, grocery store workers, and more. Those workers didn't have to worry about shelter instability, and were still able to make their monthly payments because it was affordable. Even amidst global upheaval, this investment remains low risk.

Finally, when you have a good insurance policy, the risk is even lower. I have personally witnessed the importance of a good and reliable insurance company. The Equity & Help housing portfolio is insured with one of the top insurance companies in the world, and that has made a big difference for their Housing PhilanthroInvestors.

Purpose and impact

Families who were temporarily homeless, or unable to make a down payment to own a home, now have a chance to provide a stable family unit, to invest in the pride of ownership, and improve their neighborhoods and communities. They will be physically, emotionally, and spiritually healthier than they were before, which supports the natural law of betterment.

Legacy

You will know that you're leaving behind two kinds of legacy:

a legacy of the valuable work you did while you were alive on this Earth, and a financial legacy that can benefit your children and grandchildren. The lender hat is a long-term hat that will continue producing recurring income for at least twenty years. It can even last thirty years, increasing the financing terms in your legal lending documents with the family you are supporting.

How to learn more and do more

This is a cursory overview of what to do. The model is designed to be flexible and adaptable for where you live, and how you want to operate.

If you'd like to learn more about how to do this yourself, you can review the resources at the end of this book that will point you to our website and our online course.

When I did my first Housing PhilanthroInvesting deal in 2009, I had a realization: if I was going to convert investors from traditional investing to PhilanthroInvesting, I would create a bigger impact by making it as easy as possible. Not all investors want to go through this process on their own. They have other jobs and commitments and families of their own. There was a gap between investors who wanted to have an impact on the world and opportunities for them to do so. I decided to fill that gap.

The Housing PhilanthroInvestor turn-key business I created does much of this process with you.

In short, when an investor works with Equity & Help, they name Equity & Help the trustee of their trust. This means Equity & Help will perform tasks, while you, the PhilanthroInvestor, remain the CEO, participating in all key material decisions and allowing for the company-trained staff to assist you by executing

HOUSING PHILANTHROINVESTING

your decisions.

Equity & Help provides investors with a list of foreclosed homes to choose from that have already received basic repairs; they find the family and manage the relationship with them; they draw up the contracts, and they facilitate the HappyHome process. All the while, you as the PhilanthroInvestor receive updates and photographs, and get involved in every key decision. You still have engagement, control, knowledge, enjoyment, and fulfillment, which is what real life is all about—*true financial freedom*! It saves you time and energy, so you can PhilanthroInvest in more families without having to execute your decisions, only make them, as a good CEO.

The Housing PhilanthroInvestor turn-key business was born with a mission to stabilize families and improve neighborhoods while raising the consciousness level of help in the investment world. You gain double-digit capital growth and double-digit cash on cash returns, with the added benefit of heartwarming moments. Equity & Help has been an Inc500 company for multiple years, was awarded the 83rd fastest-growing company in the United States in 2020 and third fastest-growing company in Florida, and placed third in the category of real estate companies in the United States.

The Housing PhilanthroInvestor turnkey business is a highly qualified platform, on the side of both the investors, and the company that facilitates Housing PhilanthroInvesting, which you manage from the comfort of your home. Our goal is to support investors in doing good, while also creating a return.

We've been extremely fortunate to watch over the years as families move into homes, putting love into creating a HappyHome, while investors enjoy not only the capital and profit cash flow, but also the updates from the families as they plant roses, paint decks, and prepare nurseries for children. Everyone wins—you, the family, the house, the neighborhood, the community, the world. When we achieve true financial freedom, the abundance spills over in ways we can't predict.

I've listed some resources at the end of the book to further explore the Housing PhilanthroInvestor turnkey business, that could be beneficial for you on your PhilanthroInvesting journey.

Success stories through Equity & Help

I would love to share a few stories of successful family pairings through our Housing PhilanthroInvesting company, equityandhelp.com. This will also help break down the steps of how you might do this yourself, and the impact you can have.

Equity & Help found a home located in Indiana, bought it from the bank, and did all the necessary repairs to show the house and make it sellable.

One of their PhilanthroInvestors saw the potential in this property and bought it for $40K. It was then Equity & Help's role to find the ideal family, which they did, and they sold it to them for $48K. The family was thrilled to find a house on the market at that price, and the immediate equity for the PhilanthroInvestor was $8K.

After moving in, the family got to work making improvements and repairs, increasing the home's value to $70K. They now live in a HappyHome, and in the meantime, the PhilanthroInvestor increased his own generational wealth for his family.

I have another example to share with you. Equity & Help came across a property in Ohio and matched it to one of their foreign PhilanthroInvestors. He purchased the home for $55,507, and they sold it in 113 days to a family for $68,600. This investor made $13K in 113 days with minimal effort and no landlord work, just being involved in decision-making. And because of the pride of ownership, the family has now increased the value of their asset to $131,676! All this happened in less than a year, thanks to the support of the PhilanthroInvestor and the family's repairs and finishing touches. The home has more than doubled in value from what the PhilanthroInvestor initially paid.

I love sharing these success stories of happy families fixing up their new, beautiful home and of PhilanthroInvestors receiving incredible returns on their turnkey business while doing something to help others. It reminds me of my first Housing PhilanthroInvesting venture with that family who asked for my help in 2009. And I realize how far we've come since that moment.

In another example, Equity & Help got a home from a bank in Texas. Their PhilanthroInvestor purchased it for $43K. Would you believe that they matched it to a family who bought it in only seventy days? It was barely on the market, and the sale price was $56,942. This family enjoyed making repairs and updates, and in only fourteen months the value of the home increased to $75,593. The family is really happy, and their PhilanthroInvestor is happy, given that the value is now almost two times the original price.

I have one more success story that I would like to tell you. Equity & Help acquired a home that met their criteria in Pennsylvania. Their PhilanthroInvestor bought it for $35,938. In under one year, they sold the house to a family. The family was excited about the price as well, buying it for only $44,203. The family immediately started home repairs and improvements, and in less than a year, the house's value increased to $67,500. That's nearly double the initial investment in less than a year!

Almost doubling your asset value in less than a year, with an asset of $67,500 in your trust, is tremendous. Especially when you are not monitoring it on your phone or computer all the time, not acting as a landlord, and just relaxing in your home and participating as the CEO of your Housing PhilanthroInvesting portfolio that your turnkey business owns and controls.

When we looked at Equity & Help's report during the last quarter of 2020, it revealed that they had homes in thirty-two states. They had recovered $30+ million U.S. dollars of assets from the banks, with an average equity gain of 27.2% for their PhilanthroInvestors (this being the difference between what their PhilanthroInvestors paid and what they sold the home to the family for).

They are working with PhilanthroInvestors in the U.S., Canada, Europe, and Latin America, totaling more than ten countries who pay an average PhilanthroInvestor price of $42K with an after-repair value of $69K. Incredible statistics. And as their network of PhilanthroInvestors grows, so too does the impact of the HappyHome triangle.

THE HAPPYHOME™
TRIANGLE

Who are the families?

By doing Housing PhilanthroInvesting, you're impacting actual people, with actual dreams, and passions, and contributions to their neighborhoods.

Here are some of the people who have participated in equityandhelp.com. We changed their names for privacy, but their details are purely theirs:

Frank is a firefighter. He is an ideal buyer: hard-working, independent, and no stranger to homes that need fixing. Frank recently went through a divorce that left him searching for a new home. Unfortunately, during the divorce process Frank's credit score took a hit and he had trouble securing traditional financing.

Frank's search led him to us, where he was able to purchase his new home for just $2,000 down. Even though the home needed work, Frank's experience made him an ideal candidate. He has already improved the home substantially.

Cody is a contractor, and another ideal buyer: entrepreneurial, a self-starter, and with experience in construction. Because Cody is self-employed, he had trouble securing a mortgage from his local bank due to their strict regulations. Cody had stopped searching for a home until he saw our sign for a fixer-upper for just $2,000 down. He gave us a call and decided to see the house. Though the house needed repairs, Cody's background ensured that he was more than capable of doing the work, and for a price way below ARV, Cody could not pass up the opportunity.

Mike and Lisa's lease was just about to end. They have two kids and are avid do-it-yourselfers, having built several pieces of furniture for their apartment. They both do quite well financially, but have student loan debt that did not qualify them for a bank loan. Mike and Lisa are both educated and were ready to own a home in which they could raise their family. They had a dream of customizing and remodeling, but the problem was securing funding. Getting a bank loan or private lending was a frustrating and unsuccessful process. When they found out they could finance a fixer-upper for just $2,000 down and less than $350 per month, they signed and closed within a week!

The families with whom you will work as a Housing PhilanthroInvestor are like so many people you know: educated, hard-working, parents, have careers, and some have even started their own businesses. They have found that for one reason or another, a mortgage is difficult to obtain, and so they get stuck sinking their money into rent, with no equity at the end of the day.

Now families can afford a place to call their own, and instead of allocating monthly funding to rent, they make home improvements to flooring, walls, fixtures, the yard, and more.

Take a Moment to PhilanthroInvest

How does it feel knowing there's a way an investor can make money, help families, and improve the value of houses in your community?

_____

_____

_____

_____

As you consider the eight steps to Housing Philanthro-Investing, what questions do you have? Can they be answered through research, or by accessing the additional resources at the end of the book?

_____

_____

_____

_____

What do you think about the process of having homeowners complete a checklist to create a HappyHome? Do you think it contributes to the pride of ownership?

_____

_____

_____

_____

Some PhilanthroInvestors who've worked with Equity & Help have increased their net worth an average of 27.2%, and a double-digit cash on cash return yearly after that. How do those numbers compare to your current investments?

_____

_____

_____

_____

As you consider the real examples of real people getting to live and invest in their own homes, what do you feel? Does this seem like a worthwhile endeavor, aligned with your values?

_____

_____

_____

_____

Conclusion

A legacy that matters

We are all connected. What happens on one side of the planet affects life on the other side. To me, this connectivity speaks to a responsibility between us all, no matter where we live or what we do.

When you engage in help, the benefits go beyond your feeling of fulfillment and a richer life, spilling into your legacy.

Legacy is born from how you live. It's about learning from the past, living in the present, and building for the future. The concept of legacy may remind us of the end of life, but it's not actually about that. Instead, we're talking about what we leave behind, the seal we leave on this planet, based on how we choose to live now. Legacy can be a great motivator for making purpose-driven choices in your life.

A legacy may take many forms—children, grandchildren, a business, an idea, a book, a community, a home, your financial habits, your investing habits, and the most important one: your example to others, including your kids. Our legacy has the potential to go beyond us. What kind of world will we leave when we're gone?

The two types of legacy—financial and purpose—each have their own benefits. With the former, you can rest assured that your children and grandchildren, or the beneficiaries of your net worth, will have a leg-up in life, thanks to your financial legacy. They will be able to start contributing a higher level of help to society sooner.

In this case, your legacy is the assets you are leaving behind.

We cannot take our worldly possessions with us when we die. Everything you've worked towards as an investor is now yours to pass on.

Building a secure financial future for your family doesn't happen accidentally. It takes consistency, effort, and focus over many years. It might not be easy, but the satisfaction of knowing all your dedication has benefitted your family for years to come is absolutely worth it.

When you leave a legacy of purpose, you decide what kind of world you're choosing to leave behind for your children. We have an obligation to make the future a little better than the past. By leaving behind a legacy of purpose, we not only inspire future generations to live in accordance with our example, we also ensure that the level of help they'll bring to the world builds upon what we've already created.

We leave an example of how to live, how to help, and how to give; a legacy of living for the sake of enjoyment and abundance, rather than money for the sake of money. Numbers are finite. Generosity is infinite.

PhilanthroInvesting is something you will be remembered for, something that will elevate the lives of your children, and something that will also create legacy ripples for the families you've uplifted into homeownership.

You may think that you are just investing in a house, but it's so much greater than that. You are affecting people and their neighborhoods, and the greater community at large. This does not only provide you a deep level of personal fulfillment, but it also gives you a whole different level of motivation beyond your money.

We are stewards of this world, and we have a calling to leave it better than how we found it, even if our contributions feel small. This is what PhilanthroInvesting can help us achieve during our time on this earth.

Now it's time to awaken your PhilanthroInvestor within and begin.

The Author

Ivan Anz is an Inc. 500 International Serial Entrepreneur with businesses in more than ten countries. Among them is PhilanthroInvestors, the educational certification and advisory firm that combines traditional venture capital financing with philanthropic principles, achieving social impact while returning profits for its PhilanthroInvestors. Mr. Anz's inherent thrust to "PhilanthroInvest" drove his 2014 creation of Equity & Help, a turn-key social-impact housing PhilanthroInvesting business. Equity & Help, Inc. has since placed in the Inc. 500 for three years in a row: 2018-2021; and in 2020 ranking #3 in Florida, with a three-year growth of 3,920%.

Mr. Anz's entrepreneurship emerged at age 7 when he leased his go-kart to his friends and neighbors while selling them candy. That undoubtedly set the stage for his success in the auto dealership and financing business, where at age 23, he grew his small family business into the #1 car dealership group of his native state in Argentina and went on to claim the Toyota best business practices awards for the entire Latin America and Caribbean.

While owning car dealerships is fun, Mr. Anz was eager to improve the community and saw housing development as a direct route to do so. To start, he built a residential neighborhood in his native Argentinian state. Even then, the PhilanthroInvestor concept lit the way: empower families to secure the lives they want without excessive financial burden.

Mr. Anz has since moved to the United States and focused his real estate endeavors on making homeownership possible for U.S. families that would otherwise be lifelong renters. He and his team do so while turning exceptional profits for their Housing PhilanthroInvestors, through Equity & Help, Inc., the first PhilanthroInvestors-certified firm.

Mr. Anz is intent on doing in other ten industries in need of improvement what he has proven can be done in the housing industry: Do good by doing well, using remarkably effective methods, like supporting social entrepreneurs worldwide who want to expand the PhilanthroInvestors phenomena and help shift the planet into a more positive direction. Mr. Anz has already expanded his footprint to the water and littering elimination industries and continues his path aiming for what he calls *the ideal world.* Discover the full vision at https://pi.today.

IVAN ANZ

Acknowledgments

A special thank you to Mr. Kent Davis.

Sir, I know you are now at peace and in good hands. You were a very special being in my life. You showed me that the problem I experienced in my country also needed to be fixed in the U.S., mentored me unconditionally, and provided me the basic tools to carry on a very important and crucial task in this country: to keep the American Dream of homeownership alive, which then allowed me to expand even beyond to help families across the globe. All my eternal love and admiration to you, Sir.

Thank you to the love of my life, Bella. You provide constant and unconditional support to my professional and personal dreams and give my life a whole different level of meaning.

Thank you to my parents, Rober and Soni, for showing me, since I was a little child, philanthropy and giving to others. This is something that is now a part of daily activity in life.

Thank you to my brother Kev for his support and changing his life to run our company in Argentina. His continuing efforts allowed me to come to the U.S. and develop the Philanthro-Investors Phenomena.

Thank you to Equity & Help, Inc team as the first Philanthro-Investors company in the world. You guys are all amazing beings whether in "calm waters" or when navigating a storm with me. This book would have not been possible if it were not for your support.

Thank you to the PhilanthroInvestors corporation executive team, for trusting in this vision when it was just a dream.

Lastly, thank you to all our PhilanthroInvestors, who, around the world, are willing to shift their mind and be able to see a light outside the world of just money for money and in that way start shifting the world in a more positive direction.

Thank you to all our PhilanthroInvestor Ambassadors across the globe who allow this phenomenon to grow by introducing us to amazing PhilanthroInvestors. You are rock stars!

Glossary of Terms

401(k) plan: Based on subsection 401(k) of the Internal Revenue Code, a 401(k) plan is a type of retirement account sponsored by employers that allows employees to invest pre-tax dollars from their paychecks. A 401(k) can be used to invest in real estate if the rules are followed.

1031 exchange: Section 1031 is an Internal Revenue Code (IRC) provision that defers tax on qualifying exchanges of like-kind real estate. Section 1031 is also known as the Starker Loophole. Qualifying Section 1031 exchanges are called 1031 exchanges, like-kind exchanges, or Starker exchanges. Section 1031 defers tax on properly structured 1031 exchanges. For 1031 exchanges concluded prior to December 31, 2017, like-kind property includes a broad range of real and tangible personal property held for business or investment such as franchises, art, equipment, stock in trade, securities, partnership interests, certificates of trust, and beneficial interests. For 1031 exchanges concluded after December 31, 2017, recently enacted tax legislation makes it clear that the only permissible property is a business or **investment in real estate.** *Source: Investopedia*

A

ARV (After Repair Value): The after-repair value (ARV) estimates the future value of a distressed property after it's been repaired. ARV is not a property's current value when purchased, but rather the estimated value of the property after improvements. ARV is commonly used by fix and flip investors who purchase, renovate, and sell properties within one year. We refer to any online estimate of value (such as Zillow's

"Zestimate") as ARV since those estimates don't consider the current condition of the home.

B

Bloomberg CityLab: A partnership between Bloomberg Philanthropies, the Aspen Institute, and The Atlantic, CityLab is the preeminent meeting of city leaders and the top minds in urbanism and city planning, economics, education, art, architecture, public sector innovation, community development, and business—convened with the goal of creating scalable solutions to major challenges faced by cities everywhere.

C

Cap rate (Capital rate): the ratio of Net Operating Income (NOI) to property asset value. So, for example, if a property was bought for $100,000 and generated an NOI of $10,000, then the cap rate would be $100,000/$1,000,000, or 10%.

Contract: A binding agreement between two or more persons that is enforceable by law.

Corporation, also called "Corp": A body formed and authorized by law to act as a single person although constituted by one or more persons and legally endowed with various rights and duties including the capacity of succession.

Custodian: A financial institution that holds customers' securities for safekeeping in order to minimize the risk of their theft or loss. A custodian holds securities and other assets in electronic or physical form. Since they are responsible for the safety of assets and securities that may be worth hundreds of millions or even billions of dollars, custodians generally tend to be large and reputable firms. A custodian is sometimes referred to as a "custodian bank.". *Source: Investopedia*

D

Deed: 1. A document that is the official government record of who owns the property and who owned the property in the past; 2. An action that is performed intentionally or consciously.

Do-it-yourselfer: The activity of *doing* or making something (as in woodworking or home repair) without professional training or assistance broadly: an activity in which one *does* something oneself or on one's own initiative.

Due Diligence: Reasonable steps taken by our property acquisitions department to satisfy our property quality standards before buying it. It includes title search and property market research, home inspection, etc.

E

E&H: Abbreviation for Equity & Help, Inc. (the name of our corporation).

Escrow: 1. An account where money is placed in holding pending some action being finalized or some condition being met. In E&H when money is escrowed, it means the investor has sent us money. Although it is now in our possession, it is not ours until we sign contracts and transfer ownership of a property in exchange of that money. 2. We refer to the investor's escrow as the place where we hold the investor's money that is not ours, for example, all the payments from a family to a property owned go directly into their escrow account. An investor can request money from their escrow at any time.

F

Family unit: A primary social group; parents and children.

Fannie Mae: The Federal National Mortgage Association, commonly known as Fannie Mae, is a United States government-sponsored enterprise.

Foreclosure: The legal proceedings initiated by a creditor to repossess the collateral for a loan that is in default. In the Housing PhilanthroInvestor turn-key business, in most of the states across the United Stated is not necessary as a title holder to go into a foreclosure process because there is not a mortgage into the property, you as the housing PhilanthroInvestor by being the beneficiary of the land trust where the title of the property is located owns the deed, so you don't need to foreclose it.

G

Gentrification: A process in which a poor area (as of a city) experiences an influx of middle-class or wealthy people who renovate and rebuild homes and businesses and which often results in an increase in property values and the displacement of earlier, usually poorer residents.

Grant: To bestow or transfer formally; to give the possession or title of by assigning the benefit of a trust.

Grantee: A recipient of a grant.

Grantor: A person who makes a grant in legal form.

H

Hat: Used to refer to a particular role or occupation of someone who has more than one.

Hazard insurance: Insurance that provides protection against certain risks such as storms or fires.

Home inspection: Reasonable on-site steps taken by our property acquisitions department to satisfy our property quality standards after the property passed due diligence and before buying it. It includes many on-site detailed pictures of the home and the surrounding area.

Housing PhilanthroInvestor turn-key business: Our housing investment program that allows investors to Philanthro-Invest by building their own housing portfolio and opening the doors for families to live in their own homes when otherwise they couldn't.

I

Insurance: An arrangement in which you regularly pay an insurance company an amount of money so that they will give you money if something you own is damaged, lost, or stolen.

Interest: 1. Right, title, or legal share in something; 2. Participation in advantage and responsibility; 3. A charge for borrowed money generally a percentage of the amount borrowed; 4. The profit in goods or money that is made on invested capital.

Invest: 1. To commit (money) to earn a financial return; 2. To make use of for future benefits or advantages, e.g., *invested her time wisely*; 3. To involve or engage especially emotionally, e.g., *were deeply invested in their children's lives*.

Investor: 1. One who commits (money) to earn a financial return; 2. One involved or engaged, especially emotionally.

IRA (Individual Retirement Account): An individual retirement account is an investing tool used by individuals to earn and earmark funds for retirement savings. There are several types of IRAs as of 2018: Traditional IRAs, Roth IRAs, and Self-Directed IRAs. Sometimes referred to as individual retirement arrangements, IRAs can consist of a range of financial products such as stocks, bonds, or mutual funds:

The Traditional IRA: A traditional individual retirement account (IRA) allows individuals to direct pretax income towards investments that can grow tax-deferred; no capital gains or dividend income is taxed until it is withdrawn. Individual taxpayers can contribute 100% of any earned compensation up to a specified maximum dollar amount. Contributions to a traditional IRA may be tax-deductible depending on the taxpayer's income, tax-filing status, and other factors.

Roth IRA: Named for Delaware Senator William Roth and established by the Taxpayer Relief Act of 1997, a Roth IRA is an individual retirement plan (a type of qualified retirement plan) that bears many similarities to the traditional IRA. The biggest distinction between the two is how they are taxed. Traditional IRA contributions are generally made with pretax dollars; you pay income tax when you withdraw the money from the account during retirement. Conversely, Roth IRAs are funded with after-tax dollars; the contributions are not tax deductible (although you may be able to take a tax credit of 10 to 50% of the contribution), depending on your income and life situation). But when you start withdrawing funds, qualified distributions are tax-free.

The Self-Directed IRA: A self-directed individual retirement account (SD-IRA) is an individual retirement account (IRA) in which the investor is in charge of making all the investment decisions. The self-directed IRA provides the investor with greater opportunity for asset diversification outside of the traditional stocks, bonds, and mutual funds. Self-directed IRAs can invest in real estate, private market securities, and more. All securities and investments are held in an account administered by a custodian or trustee. A self-directed IRA is a type of traditional or Roth IRA. A SD-IRA is used to save for retirement and is structured to facilitate withdrawals at a specified age. Self-directed IRAs differ from traditional and Roth IRAs only by the assets they hold. Designed for do-it-yourself investors they allow the owner to invest in a much broader array of securities than with a traditional or Roth IRA. *Source: Investopedia*

J

Jim Bunning (October 23, 1931 – May 26, 2017) was an American professional baseball pitcher and politician who represented Kentucky in both chambers of the United States Congress. He is the sole Major League Baseball athlete to have been elected to both the United States Senate and the National Baseball Hall of Fame.

L

Land contract: A real estate contract in which the buyer agrees to make periodic payments to the seller, taking title only when the purchase price has been paid in full. Mostly used in the housing industry.

LLC: Abbreviation for Limited Liability Company. This is used to simplify corporate setup, using an individual's tax filing, but offering the protection of a corporation.

Land trust: A land trust is a legal agreement in which a property owner transfers the title to a property to a trustee. The property owner is typically the beneficiary and directs the trustee in all matters relating to the management of the property, as outlined in the trust agreement or deed. The property owner also retains all property rights including the freedom to develop, rent and sell the property. One land trust example is known as a real-estate land trust. Corporations and other institutional buyers sometimes use these trusts to purchase large tracts of land to discreetly avoid publicity. Publicity might cause the price of future land purchases to increase and potentially disrupt the firm's plans for developing or profiting from the land. Individuals usually use land trusts for privacy and to avoid probate. In both cases, the trust itself is the buyer. In fact, the world-famous Walt Disney Resort in Orlando, Fl., was initially purchased by a trust. The original landowners of the Florida swamplands, where the resort now stands, had no idea, Disney, already a burgeoning company at the time, was behind the purchase. These types of trusts are often called "Illinois land trusts," because businessmen and politicians in 1800s Chicago were the first to establish the vehicle. Several politicians used these trusts to purchase land in the area and protect their roles as a city alderman because they would have been barred from voting in local city development projects as landowners in the same area. One of the main advantages of this type of trust is that the actual property owner remains anonymous. In public records, the name of the trust is the holder of the property. This type of arrangement cannot only bring some legal protection, but it can also help the property owner negotiates prices if he or she is particularly wealthy. *Source: Investopedia*

Lincoln Institute of Land Policy: A think tank based in Cambridge, MA, which seeks to improve quality of life through the effective use, taxation, and stewardship of land.

Living trust: A trust that becomes effective during the

lifetime of the settlor.

M

Mean income (average): The amount obtained by dividing the total aggregate income of a group by the number of units in that group.

Median income: The amount which divides the income distribution into two equal groups, half having income above that amount, and half having income below that amount.

Mortgage: A conveyance of or lien against property (as for securing a loan) that becomes void upon payment or performance according to stipulated terms. In the Housing PhilanthroInvestor turn-key business, there is not mortgage require to be processed because the land trust holds the deed and gives a family a land contract.

N

National Association of Realtors (NAR): American's largest trade association, representing 1.4 million members, including NAR's institutes, societies, and councils, involved in all aspects of the residential and commercial real estate industries.

P

Personal property: Everything that is the subject of ownership that does not come under the denomination of real property; any right or interest that an individual has in movable things. Personal property can be divided into two major categories: (1) corporeal personal property, including such items as animals, merchandise, and jewelry; and (2) incorporeal personal property, comprised of such rights as stocks, bonds, interests in trusts, patents, and copyrights.

Personal property trust: The "personal property trust" agreement is basically the same as a land trust in that the trustee is essentially a nominee title–holder acting at your direction. Like the land trust, the paper trust is a revocable, living trust. The same rules for tax reporting apply: there is no gift tax or income tax consequence of placing title to your paper in the paper trust. You still retain full control of your trustee, so no fiduciary tax return is required. Like the land trust, the primary purpose of using the personal property trust is to keep your name off the public records. Source: LegalWiz

PhilanthroInvestor: This is a term created by Ivan Anz: Someone who invests money and time, engaging emotionally to promote human welfare while earning a financial return.

Philanthropist: One who makes an active effort to promote human welfare.

Pro Bono: Denoting work undertaken without charge, especially legal work for a client with a low income.

Property taxes: A tax levied on the value of property.

R

Return on investment (ROI): A performance measure used to evaluate the efficiency of an investment or to compare the efficiency of a number of different investments. ROI measures the amount of return on an investment relative to the investment's cost. To calculate ROI, the benefit (or return) of an investment is divided by the cost of the investment, and the result is expressed as a percentage or a ratio. There are other calculations such as cap rate which may be referred to as an ROI.

For you to understand the difference, let's give you an example:

Investment: $100,000

Total Money Returned after investment is finalized: $200,000

Time Period of the investment: 10 Years

Yearly Income generated by the Investment: $10,000

ROI: 100% ($100,000 of Profit over $100,000 of Investment)

Cap Rate: 10% ($10,000 a year over $100,000 of Investment)

T

Trust: A legally binding document which can own assets (i.e. properties, money, stocks, etc.).

Trustee: An individual person or member of a board given control or powers of administration of property in trust with a legal obligation to administer it solely for the purposes specified. The trustee is the physical representation of the trust agreement and can sign contracts and deal with counties the way an owner of the property could.

Trustor: Is the one who contributes property to the trust. The trustee is the person who manages the trust and is usually appointed by the trustor. The trustor is also often the trustee in living trusts.

Turnkey: A turnkey, a turnkey project, or a turnkey operation is a type of project that is constructed so that it can be sold to any buyer as a completed product.

U

UN-Habitat: The United Nations program for human settlements and sustainable urban development.

Index

Learn About PhilanthroInvesting

PhilanthroInvestors.com/Learn

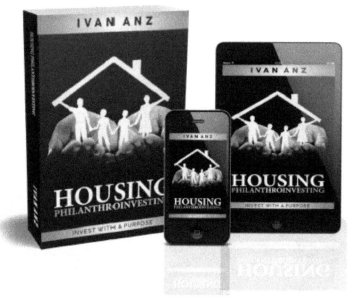

Make a Statement
Shop Our Merchandise Today

PhilanthroInvestors.com/Shop

CPSIA information can be obtained
at www.ICGtesting.com
Printed in the USA
LVHW081615020722
722532LV00019B/367/J